I0752752

BY COMMAND OF His late Majesty WILLIAM THE IVth

and under the Patronage of

Her Majesty the Queen.

HISTORICAL RECORDS,

OF THE

British Army

Comprising the

History of every Regiment

IN HER MAJESTY'S SERVICE.

By Richard Cannon Esq.re

Adjutant Generals Office Horse Guards.

London.

Printed by Authority.

THE SEVENTY-FOURTH REGIMENT
(HIGHLANDERS),

BEARS ON THE REGIMENTAL COLOUR AND APPOINTMENTS

"THE ELEPHANT,"

WITH THE WORD "ASSAYE," SUPERSCRIBED;

AND THE WORD

"SERINGAPATAM;"

IN COMMEMORATION OF ITS DISTINGUISHED GALLANTRY IN THE STORMING AND CAPTURE OF SERINGAPATAM, ON THE 4TH MAY, 1799; AND OF ITS HEROIC CONDUCT AT THE

"BATTLE OF ASSAYE"

ON THE 23RD SEPTEMBER 1803:

ALSO THE WORDS

"BUSACO," "FUENTES D'ONOR," "CIUDAD RODRIGO," "BADAJOZ," "SALAMANCA," "VITTORIA," "PYRENEES," "NIVELLE," "ORTHES," "TOULOUSE," AND "PENINSULA,"

IN TESTIMONY OF ITS ARDUOUS SERVICES IN PORTUGAL, SPAIN, AND FRANCE, FROM 1810 TO 1814.

The Naval & Military Press

Published by

The Naval & Military Press Ltd

Unit 5 Riverside, Brambleside
Bellbrook Industrial Estate
Uckfield, East Sussex
TN22 1QQ England

Tel: +44 (0)1825 749494

www.naval-military-press.com
www.nmarchive.com

GENERAL ORDERS.

HORSE-GUARDS,
1st January, 1836.

HIS MAJESTY has been pleased to command that, with the view of doing the fullest justice to Regiments, as well as to Individuals who have distinguished themselves by their Bravery in Action with the Enemy, an Account of the Services of every Regiment in the British Army shall be published under the superintendence and direction of the Adjutant-General; and that this Account shall contain the following particulars, viz.:—

—— The Period and Circumstances of the Original Formation of the Regiment; The Stations at which it has been from time to time employed; The Battles, Sieges, and other Military Operations in which it has been engaged, particularly specifying any Achievement it may have performed, and the Colours, Trophies, &c., it may have captured from the Enemy.

—— The Names of the Officers, and the number of Non-Commissioned Officers and Privates Killed or Wounded by the Enemy, specifying the place and Date of the Action.

—— The Names of those Officers who, in consideration of their Gallant Services and Meritorious Conduct in Engagements with the Enemy, have been distinguished with Titles, Medals, or other Marks of His Majesty's gracious favour.

—— The Names of all such Officers, Non-Commissioned Officers, and Privates, as may have specially signalized themselves in Action.

And,

—— The Badges and Devices which the Regiment may have been permitted to bear, and the Causes on account of which such Badges or Devices, or any other Marks of Distinction, have been granted.

By Command of the Right Honorable

GENERAL LORD HILL,

Commanding-in-Chief.

JOHN MACDONALD,

Adjutant-General.

PREFACE.

The character and credit of the British Army must chiefly depend upon the zeal and ardour by which all who enter into its service are animated, and consequently it is of the highest importance that any measure calculated to excite the spirit of emulation, by which alone great and gallant actions are achieved, should be adopted.

Nothing can more fully tend to the accomplishment of this desirable object than a full display of the noble deeds with which the Military History of our country abounds. To hold forth these bright examples to the imitation of the youthful soldier, and thus to incite him to emulate the meritorious conduct of those who have preceded him in their honorable career, are among the motives that have given rise to the present publication.

The operations of the British Troops are, indeed, announced in the "London Gazette," from whence they are transferred into the public prints: the achievements of our armies are thus made known at the time of their occurrence, and receive the tribute of praise and admiration to which they are entitled. On extraordinary occasions, the Houses of Parliament have been in the habit of conferring on the Commanders, and the Officers and Troops acting under their orders, expressions of approbation and of thanks for their skill and bravery; and these testimonials, confirmed by the high honour of their Sovereign's approbation, constitute the reward which the soldier most highly prizes.

It has not, however, until late years, been the practice (which appears to have long prevailed in some of the Continental armies) for British Regiments to keep regular records of their services and achievements. Hence some difficulty has been experienced in obtaining, particularly from the old Regiments, an authentic account of their origin and subsequent services.

This defect will now be remedied, in consequence of His Majesty having been pleased to command that every Regiment shall, in future, keep a full and ample record of its services at home and abroad.

From the materials thus collected, the country will henceforth derive information as to the difficulties and privations which chequer the career of those who embrace the military profession. In Great Britain, where so large a number of persons are devoted to the active concerns of agriculture, manufactures, and commerce, and where these pursuits have, for so long a period, being undisturbed by the *presence of war*, which few other countries have escaped, comparatively little is known of the vicissitudes of active service and of the casualties of climate, to which, even during peace, the British Troops are exposed in every part of the globe, with little or no interval of repose.

In their tranquil enjoyment of the blessings which the country derives from the industry and the enterprise of the agriculturist and the trader, its happy inhabitants may be supposed not often to reflect on the perilous duties of the soldier and the sailor,—on their sufferings,—and on the sacrifice of valuable life, by which so many national benefits are obtained and preserved.

The conduct of the British Troops, their valour, and endurance, have shone conspicuously under great and trying difficulties; and their character has been established in Continental warfare by the irresistible spirit with which they have effected debarkations in spite of the most formidable opposition, and by the gallantry and steadiness with which they have maintained their advantages against superior numbers.

In the official Reports made by the respective Commanders, ample justice has generally been done to the gallant exertions of the Corps employed; but the details of their services and of acts of individual bravery can only be fully given in the Annals of the various Regiments.

These Records are now preparing for publication, under His Majesty's special authority, by Mr. RICHARD CANNON, Principal Clerk of the Adjutant General's Office; and while the perusal of them cannot fail to be useful and interesting to military men of every rank, it is considered that they will also afford entertainment and information to the general reader, particularly to those who may have served in the Army, or who have relatives in the Service.

There exists in the breasts of most of those who have served, or are serving, in the Army, an *Esprit de Corps*—an attachment to everything belonging to their Regiment; to such persons a narrative of the services of their own Corps cannot fail to prove interesting. Authentic accounts of the actions of the great, the valiant, the loyal, have always been of paramount interest with a brave and civilized people. Great Britain has produced a race of heroes who, in moments of danger and terror, have stood "firm as the rocks of their native shore:" and when half the world has been arrayed against them, they have fought the battles of their Country with unshaken fortitude. It is presumed that a record of achievements in war,—victories so complete and surprising, gained by our countrymen, our brothers, our fellow citizens in arms,—a record which revives the memory of the brave, and brings their gallant deeds before us,—will certainly prove acceptable to the public.

Biographical Memoirs of the Colonels and other distinguished Officers will be introduced in the Records of their respective Regiments, and the Honorary Distinctions which have, from time to time, been conferred upon each Regiment, as testifying the value and importance of its services, will be faithfully set forth.

As a convenient mode of Publication, the Record of each Regiment will be printed in a distinct number, so that when the whole shall be completed, the Parts may be bound up in numerical succession.

INTRODUCTION

TO

THE INFANTRY.

THE natives of Britain have, at all periods, been celebrated for innate courage and unshaken firmness, and the national superiority of the British troops over those of other countries has been evinced in the midst of the most imminent perils. History contains so many proofs of extraordinary acts of bravery, that no doubts can be raised upon the facts which are recorded. It must therefore be admitted, that the distinguishing feature of the British soldier is INTREPIDITY. This quality was evinced by the inhabitants of England when their country was invaded by Julius Cæsar with a Roman army, on which occasion the undaunted Britons rushed into the sea to attack the Roman soldiers as they descended from their ships; and, although their discipline and arms were inferior to those of their adversaries, yet their fierce and dauntless bearing intimidated the flower of the Roman troops, including Cæsar's favourite tenth legion. Their arms consisted of spears, short swords, and other weapons of rude construction. They had chariots, to the axles of which were fastened sharp pieces of iron resembling scythe-blades, and infantry in long chariots resembling waggons, who alighted and fought on foot, and for change of ground, pursuit or retreat, sprang into the chariot and drove off with the speed of cavalry. These inventions were, however, unavailing against Cæsar's legions: in the course of time a military system, with discipline and subordination, was introduced, and British courage, being thus regulated, was exerted to the greatest advantage; a full development of the national character followed, and it shone forth in all its native brilliancy.

The military force of the Anglo-Saxons consisted principally of infantry: Thanes, and other men of property, however, fought on horseback. The infantry were of two classes, heavy and light. The former carried large shields armed with spikes, long broad swords and spears; and the latter were armed with swords or spears only. They had also men armed with clubs, others with battle-axes and javelins.

The feudal troops established by William the Conqueror consisted (as already stated in the Introduction to the Cavalry) almost entirely of horse; but when the warlike barons and knights, with their trains of tenants and vassals, took the field, a proportion of men appeared on foot, and, although these were of inferior degree, they proved stout-hearted Britons of stanch fidelity. When stipendiary troops were employed, infantry always constituted a considerable portion of the military force;

and this *arme* has since acquired, in every quarter of the globe, a celebrity never exceeded by the armies of any nation at any period.

The weapons carried by the infantry, during the several reigns succeeding the Conquest, were bows and arrows, half-pikes, lances, halberds, various kinds of battle-axes, swords, and daggers. Armour was worn on the head and body, and in course of time the practice became general for military men to be so completely cased in steel, that it was almost impossible to slay them.

The introduction of the use of gunpowder in the destructive purposes of war, in the early part of the fourteenth century, produced a change in the arms and equipment of the infantry-soldier. Bows and arrows gave place to various kinds of fire-arms, but British archers continued formidable adversaries; and, owing to the inconvenient construction and imperfect bore of the fire-arms when first introduced, a body of men, well trained in the use of the bow from their youth, was considered a valuable acquisition to every army, even as late as the sixteenth century.

During a great part of the reign of Queen Elizabeth each company of infantry usually consisted of men armed five different ways; in every hundred men forty were "*men-at-arms*," and sixty "*shot*;" the "men-at-arms" were ten halberdiers, or battle-axe men, and thirty pikemen; and the "shot" were twenty archers, twenty musketeers, and twenty harquebusiers, and each man carried, besides his principal weapon, a sword and dagger.

Companies of infantry varied at this period in numbers from 150 to 300 men; each company had a colour or ensign, and the mode of formation recommended by an English military writer (Sir John Smithe) in 1590 was:—the colour in the centre of the company guarded by the halberdiers; the pikemen in equal proportions, on each flank of the halberdiers: half the musketeers on each flank of the pikes; half the archers on each flank of the musketeers, and the harquebusiers (whose arms were much lighter than the muskets then in use) in equal proportions on each flank of the company for skirmishing.* It was customary to unite a number of companies into one body, called a REGIMENT, which frequently amounted to three thousand men: but each company continued to carry a colour. Numerous improvements were eventually introduced in the construction of fire-arms, and, it having been found impossible to make armour proof against the muskets then in use (which carried a very heavy ball) without its being too weighty for the soldier, armour was gradually laid aside by the infantry in the seventeenth century: bows and arrows also fell into disuse, and the infantry were reduced to two classes, viz.: *musketeers*, armed with matchlock muskets,

---

* A company of 200 men would appear thus:—

20	20	20	30	20	30	20	20	20
Harquebuses.	Archers.	Muskets.	Pikes.	Halberds.	Pikes.	Muskets.	Archers.	Harquebuses.

The musket carried a ball which weighed $\frac{1}{10}$th of a pound; and the harquebus a ball which weighed $\frac{1}{23}$th of a pound.

swords, and daggers; and *pikemen*, armed with pikes from fourteen to eighteen feet long, and swords.

In the early part of the seventeenth century Gustavus Adolphus, King of Sweden, reduced the strength of regiments to 1000 men. He caused the gunpowder, which had heretofore been carried in flasks, or in small wooden bandoliers, each containing a charge, to be made up into cartridges, and carried in pouches; and he formed each regiment into two wings of musketeers, and a centre division of pikemen. He also adopted the practice of forming four regiments into a brigade; and the number of colours was afterwards reduced to three in each regiment. He formed his columns so compactly that his infantry could resist the charge of the celebrated Polish horsemen and Austrian cuirassiers; and his armies became the admiration of other nations. His mode of formation was copied by the English, French, and other European states; but so great was the prejudice in favour of ancient customs, that all his improvements were not adopted until near a century afterwards.

In 1664 King Charles II. raised a corps for sea-service, styled the Admiral's regiment. In 1678 each company of 100 men usually consisted of 30 pikemen, 60 musketeers, and 10 men armed with light firelocks. In this year the King added a company of men armed with hand grenades to each of the old British regiments, which was designated the "grenadier company." Daggers were so contrived as to fit in the muzzles of the muskets, and bayonets, similar to those at present in use, were adopted about twenty years afterwards.

An Ordnance regiment was raised in 1685, by order of King James II., to guard the artillery, and was designated the Royal Fusiliers (now 7th Foot). This corps, and the companies of grenadiers, did not carry pikes

King William III. incorporated the Admiral's regiment in the second Foot Guards, and raised two Marine regiments for sea-service. During the war in this reign, each company of infantry (excepting the fusiliers and grenadiers) consisted of 14 pikemen and 46 musketeers; the captains carried pikes; lieutenants, partisans; ensigns, half-pikes; and serjeants, halberds. After the peace in 1697 the Marine regiments were disbanded, but were again formed on the breaking out of the war in 1702.*

During the reign of Queen Anne the pikes were laid aside, and every infantry soldier was armed with a musket, bayonet, and sword; the grenadiers ceased, about the same period, to carry hand grenades; and the regiments were directed to lay aside their third colour: the corps of Royal Artillery was first added to the Army in this reign.

About the year 1745, the men of the battalion companies of infantry ceased to carry swords; during

* The 30th, 31st, and 32nd Regiments were formed as Marine corps in 1702, and were employed as such during the wars in the reign of Queen Anne. The Marine corps were embarked in the Fleet under Admiral Sir George Rooke, and were at the taking of Gibraltar, and in its subsequent defence in 1704; they were afterwards employed at the siege of Barcelona in 1705.

the reign of George II. light companies were added to infantry regiments; and in 1764 a Board of General Officers recommended that the grenadiers should lay aside their swords, as that weapon had never been used during the Seven Years' War. Since that period the arms of the infantry soldier have been limited to the musket and bayonet.

The arms and equipment of the British Troops have seldom differed materially, since the Conquest, from those of other European states; and in some respects the arming has, at certain periods, been allowed to be inferior to that of the nations with whom they have had to contend; yet, under this disadvantage, the bravery and superiority of the British infantry have been evinced on very many and most trying occasions, and splendid victories have been gained over very superior numbers.

Great Britain has produced a race of lion-like champions who have dared to confront a host of foes, and have proved themselves valiant with any arms. At *Crecy*, King Edward III., at the head of about 30,000 men, defeated, on the 26th of August, 1346, Philip King of France, whose army is said to have amounted to 100,000 men; here British valour encountered veterans of renown:—the King of Bohemia, the King of Majorca, and many princes and nobles were slain, and the French army was routed and cut to pieces. Ten years afterwards, Edward Prince of Wales, who was designated the Black Prince, defeated, at *Poictiers*, with 14,000 men, a French army of 60,000 horse, besides infantry, and took John I., King of France, and his son

Philip, prisoners. On the 25th of October, 1415, King Henry V., with an army of about 13,000 men, although greatly exhausted by marches, privations, and sickness, defeated, at *Agincourt*, the Constable of France, at the head of the flower of the French nobility and an army said to amount to 60,000 men, and gained a complete victory.

During the seventy years' war between the United Provinces of the Netherlands and the Spanish monarchy, which commenced in 1578 and terminated in 1648, the British infantry in the service of the States-General were celebrated for their unconquerable spirit and firmness;* and in the thirty years' war between the Protestant Princes and the Emperor of Germany, the British Troops in the service of Sweden and other states were celebrated for deeds of heroism.† In the wars of Queen Anne, the fame of the British army under the great MARLBOROUGH was spread throughout the world; and if we glance at the achievements performed within the memory of persons now living, there is abundant proof that the Britons of the present age are not inferior to their ancestors in the qualities

---

* The brave Sir Roger Williams, in his Discourse on War, printed in 1590, observes:—"I persuade myself ten thousand of our nation would beat thirty thousand of theirs (the Spaniards) out of the field, let them be chosen where they list." Yet at this time the Spanish infantry was allowed to be the best disciplined in Europe. For instances of valour displayed by the British Infantry during the Seventy Years' War, see the Historical Record of the Third Foot, or Buffs.

† *Vide* the Historical Record of the First, or Royal Regiment of Foot.

which constitute good soldiers. Witness the deeds of the brave men, of whom there are many now surviving, who fought in Egypt in 1801, under the brave Abercromby, and compelled the French army, which had been vainly styled *Invincible*, to evacuate that country; also the services of the gallant Troops during the arduous campaigns in the Peninsula, under the immortal WELLINGTON; and the determined stand made by the British Army at Waterloo, where Napoleon Bonaparte, who had long been the inveterate enemy of Great Britain, and had sought and planned her destruction by every means he could devise, was compelled to leave his vanquished legions to their fate, and to place himself at the disposal of the British Government. These achievements, with others of recent dates, in the distant climes of India, prove that the same valour and constancy which glowed in the breasts of the heroes of Crecy, Poictiers, Agincourt, Blenheim, and Ramilies, continue to animate the Britons of the nineteenth century.

The British Soldier is distinguished for a robust and muscular frame,—intrepidity which no danger can appal,—unconquerable spirit and resolution,—patience in fatigue and privation, and cheerful obedience to his superiors. These qualities, united with an excellent system of order and discipline to regulate and give a skilful direction to the energies and adventurous spirit of the hero, and a wise selection of officers of superior talent to command, whose presence inspires confidence,—have been the leading causes of the splendid victories gained by the British arms.* The fame of the deeds of the past and present generations in the various battle-fields where the robust sons of Albion have fought and conquered, surrounds the British arms with a halo of glory; these achievements will live in the page of history to the end of time.

The records of the several regiments will be found to contain a detail of facts of an interesting character, connected with the hardships, sufferings, and gallant exploits of British soldiers in the various parts of the world where the calls of their Country and the commands of their Sovereign have required them to proceed in the execution of their duty, whether in

---

* Under the blessing of Divine Providence, His Majesty ascribes the successes which have attended the exertions of his troops in Egypt to that determined bravery which is inherent in Britons; but His Majesty desires it may be most solemnly and forcibly impressed on the consideration of every part of the army, that it has been a strict observance of order, discipline, and military system, which has given the full energy to the native valour of the troops, and has enabled them proudly to assert the superiority of the national military character, in situations uncommonly arduous, and under circumstances of peculiar difficulty."—*General Orders in* 1801.

In the General Orders issued by Lieut.-General Sir John Hope (afterwards Lord Hopetoun), congratulating the army upon the successful result of the Battle of Corunna, on the 16th of January, 1809, it is stated:—"On no occasion has the undaunted valour of British troops ever been more manifest. At the termination of a severe and harassing march, rendered necessary by the superiority which the enemy had acquired, and which had materially impaired the efficiency of the troops, many disadvantages were to be encountered. These have all been surmounted by the conduct of the troops themselves: and the enemy has been taught, that whatever advantages of position or of numbers he may possess, there is inherent in the British officers and soldiers a bravery that knows not how to yield,—that no circumstances can appal,—and that will ensure victory, when it is to be obtained by the exertion of any human means."

active continental operations, or in maintaining colonial territories in distant and unfavourable climes.

The superiority of the British Infantry has been pre-eminently set forth in the wars of six centuries, and admitted by the greatest commanders which Europe has produced. The formations and movements of this *armé*, as at present practised, while they are adapted to every species of warfare, and to all probable situations and circumstances of service, are calculated to show forth the brilliancy of military tactics calculated upon mathematical and scientific principles. Although the movements and evolutions have been copied from the continental armies, yet various improvements have from time to time been introduced, to ensure that simplicity and celerity by which the superiority of the national military character is maintained. The rank and influence which Great Britain has attained among the nations of the world, have in a great measure been purchased by the valour of the Army, and to persons who have the welfare of their country at heart, the records of the several regiments cannot fail to prove interesting.

THE SEVENTY-FOURTH REGIMENT, (HIGHLANDERS.)

CONTENTS

OF THE

HISTORICAL RECORD.

PLATES.

SUCCESSION OF COLONELS

OF

THE SEVENTY-FOURTH REGIMENT

(HIGHLANDERS).

CONTENTS OF APPENDIX

TO

THE SEVENTY-FOURTH REGIMENT

(HIGHLANDERS).

SEVENTY FOURTH HIGHLANDERS.

1787.

FOR CANNON'S MILITARY RECORDS.

HISTORICAL RECORD

OF

THE SEVENTY-FOURTH REGIMENT,

(HIGHLANDERS.)

In the year 1787, apprehensions were entertained, that the affairs of Holland would involve Europe in war. Great disturbances had occurred in Holland, fomented and encouraged by the French party, who wished to expel the Stadtholder, under the supposition that he had counteracted the views of the Dutch, which were intended to have promoted the interest of France during the American war. The French court, however, intimated, that it did not intend to interfere in these disputes, except as a mediator, provided other Powers observed the same moderation; but England and Prussia having determined to take a more decisive part, caused immediate preparations to be made for hostilities. 1787

The British Minister, among other measures, proposed to augment the army in India by raising four King's regiments (the present Seventy-fourth, seventy-fifth, seventy-sixth, and seventy-seventh), the expenses of which were to be defrayed by the East India Company. The proposal was, in the first instance, readily accepted; but the threatenings of war passed over on the termination of the disputes between the Stadtholder and the United Provinces. The Court of

1787 Directors discovering that it was intended to continue these regiments as a permanent charge upon their establishment, resolutely withdrew their consent, refusing even permission to embark the troops on board their ships. These circumstances induced Mr. Pitt, the Prime Minister in the year 1788, to introduce the *Declaratory Bill,* intended to define the true meaning of his INDIA BILL of 1784, the power of the Board of Control having been disputed by the East India Company, which had refused to pay the cost of the four regiments embarked for India. After a lengthened debate, the *Declaratory Bill* was passed, by which it was directed, that the "Expense of raising, transporting, and maintaining such troops as may be judged necessary for the security of the British Territories and Possessions in the East Indies, should be defrayed out of the Revenues arising from the said territories and possessions." A further Act on the subject was passed in the year 1791, and both these Acts were confirmed by that of the 33rd of King George III., chapter 52, dated the 11th of June 1793.

The SEVENTY-FOURTH HIGHLAND REGIMENT* which

---

* In April 1758, the Second Battalions of fifteen regiments of infantry, between the 3rd and the 37th, were directed to be formed into distinct regiments, and numbered from the 61st to the 75th successively. The second battalion of the *Thirty-sixth* regiment was constituted the SEVENTY-FOURTH regiment; and was disbanded in the year 1763, after the peace of Fontainebleau.

Soon after the commencement of the American war, a regiment was authorised to be raised in the Highlands by Colonel John Campbell of Barbreck, in the year 1777, for service in America, where it was employed until the conclusion of the war in 1783, when it was disbanded.

The present SEVENTY-FOURTH regiment was formed in the year 1787, and was raised in Scotland, under the circumstances explained in the Historical Record.

is now borne on the present establishment of the army, 1787
was raised at Glasgow in the year 1787, and chiefly composed of recruits from the Highlands, by Major-General Sir Archibald Campbell, K. B. (from the half-pay of Fraser's Highlanders) whose commission, as Colonel of the SEVENTY-FOURTH, was dated the 12th October 1787.—

The establishment of the regiment was fixed at ten companies, consisting of

1 Colonel and Captain	30 Serjeants
1 Lieut.-Colonel and Captain	40 Corporals
1 Major and Captain	20 Drummers
7 Captains	2 Fifers, and
1 Captain-Lieutenant	710 Privates
21 Lieutenants	
8 Ensigns	
1 Chaplain	
1 Adjutant	
1 Quarter-master	
1 Surgeon	
2 Surgeon's Mates	

A recruiting company was afterwards added, which consisted of—

1 Captain
2 Lieutenants
1 Ensign
8 Serjeants
8 Corporals
4 Drummers
30 Privates

Total of Officers and Men of all ranks 902.

The Regiment was styled "THE SEVENTY-FOURTH, HIGHLAND, REGIMENT OF FOOT;" the Uniform was the full Highland garb of kilt and feathered bonnet, the tartan being similar to that of the forty-second regiment, and the facings white; the use of the kilt was however discontinued in the East Indies, as being unsuited to the climate.

1787 The following were the officers first appointed to the Regiment:—

RANK.	NAMES.	Commissions dated	
		In Regiment.	In Army.
Colonel .	Archibald Campbell, K. B.*	12 Oct. 1787	12 Nov. 1782
Lieut.-Col.	Gordon Forbes . .	,, ,,	24 Sept. 1781
Major . .	.. ..	..	..
Captain .	Dugald Campbell .	25 Dec. 1787	17 Oct. 1779
,,	Alexander Campbell	,, ,,	13 April 1780
,,	Archibald Campbell.	,, ,,	30 June 1781
,,	William Wallace .	,, ,,	13 Feb. 1783
,,	Robert Wood . .	,, ,,	20 Dec. 1785
Cap.-Lieut. and Capt.	Heneage Twysden .	,, ,,	
Lieutenant	James Clark. . .	,, ,,	Capt. 8 Dec. 1780
,,	Charles Campbell .	,, ,,	19 July 1780
,,	John Campbell . .	,, ,,	1 Sept. 1781
,,	Thomas Carnie . .	,, ,,	25 Oct. 1781
,,	W. Coningsby Davies	,, ,,	21 Feb. 1783
,,	Dugald Lamont .	,, ,,	6 July 1784
,,	John Alexander. .	,, ,,	5 Oct. 1785
,,	Samuel Swinton. .	,, ,,	,, ,,
,,	John Campbell . .	,, ,,	,, ,,
,,	Charles Campbell .	,, ,,	,, ,,
,,	Geo. Hy. Vansittart.	,, ,,	,, ,,
,,	Archibald Campbell	,, ,,	,, ,,
Ensign .	John Forbes . . .	,, ,,	,, ,,
,,	Alexander Stewart .	26 Dec. 1787	,, ,,
,,	James Campbell. .	27 Dec. 1787	,, ,,
,,	John Wallace . .	28 Dec. 1787	,, ,,
,,	Hugh Mc Pherson .	29 Dec. 1787	,, ,,
Chaplain .	John Ferguson . .	25 Dec. 1787	,, ,,
Adjutant .	Samuel Swinton . .	,, ,,	,, ,,
Quar.-Mas.	James Clark . .	,, ,,	,, ,,
Surgeon .	William Henderson.	,, ,,	,, ,,

1788 As the call for reinforcements to India was urgent, orders were issued to embody as many men as had been raised previous to January 1788, without waiting for the full complement; accordingly about four hundred men were assembled at Glasgow, and marched to Grangemouth, whence they embarked for Chatham, and sailed for the East Indies under Captain William Wallace; Lieut.-Colonel Forbes and the Staff remain-

* See note inserted in Appendix No. 1, page 125.

ing to recruit the Regiment to the full establishment. 1788
This being accomplished in the autumn of the same year, the Head Quarters and six companies, in
February 1789, followed the former detachment, and 1789
after a passage of four months, during which they enjoyed perfect health, landed at Madras in June 1789. The Regiment was united and stationed at the cantonments of Poonamalee, forming a corps of 750 rank and file, in every respect complete and fit for service.

Lieut.-Colonel Hamilton Maxwell, who had succeeded Lieut.-Colonel Forbes in command of the Regiment on the 3rd November 1788, was indefatigable in training it to a uniform system, impressing upon officers and men a tone and discipline to which the extraordinarily high character and success of the corps throughout its service in India was mainly attributable.

The Regiment took the field in the year 1790, and at 1790
Arnee, in the month of September, joined the centre division of the army, assembled under the orders of Major-General Medows for operations against Tippoo, Sultan of Mysore. Lieut.-Colonel Maxwell commanded this division, which advanced into the Baramhal country on the 24th October, proceeding as far as Kistnagherry and Caverypatam, and was engaged in various skirmishes with Tippoo's army until the 17th November, when the division was united with the remainder of the army under the immediate command of Major-General Medows.

The Marquis Cornwallis, Governor-General and Commander in Chief, having arrived at Madras, in September 1790, assumed the command of the army, and was at Velout, eighteen miles from Madras, on the 29th January 1791.

The Seventy-fourth was then formed with the 1791

1791 seventy-first and seventy-second regiments, into the second European Brigade, under Lieut.-Colonel Clarke, in the left wing of the army, which commenced its march from Velout on the 5th of February; and turning the Pass of Amboor, reached the table land of Mysore by the Pass of Mooglee on the 20th of February. It arrived before *Bangalore* on the 5th of March, which fortress was taken by storm on the 21st of March.

In the orders of the following day it was stated,—"Lord Cornwallis feels the most sensible gratification "in congratulating the officers and soldiers of the "army on the honorable issue of the fatigues and "dangers they have undergone during the late arduous "siege. Their alacrity and firmness in the execution "of their various duties have perhaps never been ex-"ceeded, and he shall not only think it incumbent on "him to represent their meritorious conduct in the "strongest colours, but he shall ever remember it with "the sincerest esteem and admiration."

In consequence of the decease of Major-General Sir Archibald Campbell, in the year 1791, Major-General Sir Charles O'Hara was removed from the Twenty-second regiment to the SEVENTY-FOURTH HIGHLANDERS on the 1st April of that year.

The army commenced its advance from Bangalore on the 4th of May, attacked and defeated the army of Tippoo in its strong position before Seringapatam on the 15th of May; but being unable to besiege the place, in consequence of the want of provisions and the state of the weather, it was ordered to commence its retreat upon Bangalore on the 26th of May.

Before commencing the retreat, the soldiers were thanked in orders by the Marquis Cornwallis for their conduct throughout these services, and it was added,—

"So long as there were any hopes of reducing 1791
"Seringapatam before the commencement of the heavy "rains, the Commander-in-Chief thought himself "happy in availing himself of their willing services; "but the unexpected bad weather for some time ex- "perienced. having rendered the attack of the enemy's "capital impracticable until the conclusion of the "ensuing monsoons, Lord Cornwallis thought he "should make an ill return for the zeal and alacrity "exhibited by the soldiers, if he desired them to draw "the guns and stores back to a magazine, where there "remains an ample supply of both, which was captured "by their valour; he did not therefore hesitate to order "the guns and stores, which were not wanted for field "service, to be destroyed."

The army commenced its march on the 26th of May, but being joined by the allied Mahratta forces on that day, continued to retreat very slowly to Bangalore, which it reached in the beginning of July; it was engaged in various operations, and in taking several hill forts in the neighbouring country. The SEVENTY-FOURTH was detached from the army at Nundydroog on the 21st of October, with three Sepoy battalions and some field artillery, under Lieut.-Colonel Maxwell, into the Baramhal country, which this column was ordered to clear of the enemy. They reached the south end of the valley by forced marches, and took the strong fort of Penagra by escalade on the 31st of October, and after scouring the whole of the Baramhal to the southward, returned towards Caverypatam, and encamped within five miles of the strong fort of Kistnagherry on the 7th of November; Lieut.-Colonel Maxwell determined on attacking the lower fort and town immediately, and the column advanced from the camp to

1791 the attack in three divisions at ten o'clock on that night; two of these were sent to the right and left to attack the lower fort on the western and eastern sides, while the centre division advanced directly towards the front wall; the divisions approached close to the walls before they were discovered, succeeded in escalading them, and got possession of the gates. The enemy fled to the upper fort without much resistance, and the original object of the attack was thus gained; but a most gallant attempt was made by Captain Wallace of the SEVENTY-FOURTH, who commanded the right division, to carry the almost inaccessible upper fort also. His division rushed up in pursuit of the fugitives, and notwithstanding the length and steepness of the ascent, his advanced party followed the enemy so closely that they had barely time to shut the gates. Their standard was taken on the steps of the gateway; but as the ladders had not been brought forward in time, it was impossible to escalade before the enemy recovered from their panic.

During two hours, repeated trials were made to get the ladders up, but the enemy hurling down showers of rocks and stones into the road, broke the ladders and crushed those who carried them; unluckily a clear moonlight discovered every movement, and at length the ladders being all destroyed, and many officers and men disabled in carrying them, Lieut.-Colonel Maxwell found it necessary to order a discontinuance of the assault.

The retreat of the men who had reached the gate, and of the rest of the troops, was conducted with such regularity, that a party, which sallied from the fort in pursuit of them, was immediately driven back. The pettah, or lower town, was set fire to, and the troops withdrawn to their camp before daylight on the 8th of November. 1791

The following were the casualties in the regiment on this occasion:—

Killed	2 Officers	1 Sergeant	5 Rank and File
Wounded	3 ,,	47 Non-commissioned officers and men	

Officers Killed.	*Officers Wounded.*
Lieutenant Forbes	Captain Wallace
,, Lamont	Lieutenant M'Kenzie
	,, Aytone

The column having also reduced several small forts in the district of Oussoor, rejoined the army on the 30th of November.

The following order was issued by the Marquis Cornwallis on the return of the column:—

"*Camp, Kingerry,*
December 1*st*, 1791.

"GENERAL ORDER,

"Lord Cornwallis returns his best thanks to Lieut.-"Colonel Maxwell for the zealous and able manner "in which he has executed his general instructions, "to dislodge and drive out the detachments that the "enemy had sent into the Baramhal and the district of "Oussoor.

"The good conduct and gallantry which was mani-"fested at the assault of Penagra, reflect great credit "upon Lieut.-Colonel Maxwell and the corps under "his command; but his Lordship considers the spirited "and judicious attempt which, after surprising and "carrying the pettah and lower fort, was made upon "the upper fort of Kistnagherry, as highly honourable to "all the officers and men who were employed on that "occasion, and justly deserving his warmest applause."

The army advanced from Hoolia Droog upon Seringapatam on the 1st of February, 1792. 1792

1792 During the successful attack and carrying of the lines before Seringapatam on the night of the 6th of February, the regiment formed part of the centre column, which was composed of the fifty-second, seventy-first, and SEVENTY-FOURTH King's regiments under Colonel Stewart (Lieut.-Colonel Maxwell of the SEVENTY-FOURTH being employed in command of the left column of the army,) with which column the Marquis Cornwallis, Commanding-in-Chief, was personally present during the action: nearly at its close, and during the confusion consequent on a night attack, Major Skelly, with the greater part of the SEVENTY-FOURTH, and also the other regiments of the centre column, having been pushed far in advance, Captain Dugald Campbell was left in command of the remaining companies of the regiment, with a small party of the fifty-second, when a sudden and formidable onset being made upon the position by a strong force of the enemy, the safety of the Commander-in-Chief, and of the centre of the army, was preserved by a gallant charge made upon the enemy by Captain Campbell, for which he and the small body under his command were highly applauded.

The casualties in the regiment on this occasion were:—

Killed	2	Rank and File.
Wounded, 2 Officers, 1 serjeant .	17	,, ,,
Missing	6	,, ,,

Officers Wounded.

Lieutenant Farquhar.
Ensign Hamilton.

In the General Order issued on the 7th of February, it was stated:—

"The conduct and valour of the officers and soldiers "of the army have often merited Lord Cornwallis's

"encomiums, but the zeal and gallantry which were so 1792
"successfully displayed last night in the attack of the "enemy's whole army, in a position which had cost him "much time and labour to fortify, can never be suffi- "ciently praised, and his Lordship's satisfaction, on an "occasion which promised to be attended with the most "substantial advantages, has been greatly heightened "by hearing from the Commanding Officers of divisions "that the meritorious behaviour was universal through "all ranks, in a degree that has rarely been equalled: "Lord Cornwallis therefore requests that the army in "general will accept of his most cordial thanks for the "noble and gallant manner in which they have exe- "cuted the plan of the attack; it covers themselves "with honour, and will ever command his warmest "sentiments of admiration."

After considerable progress had been made in the preparations for the siege of Seringapatam, and the second parallel completed, the operations were suspended on the 24th of February in consequence of nego- ciations for a treaty of peace, which was finally concluded with Tippoo, and the army evacuated the island of Seringapatam about the end of March, 1792. The regiment returned to cantonments in the neighbour- hood of Madras in the month of May.

The regiment was again ordered on active service 1793
against the French settlement of Pondicherry in June, 1793, being formed in brigade with the seventy-second and seventy-third regiments, and the third Company's European regiment, under Colonel Braithwaite. The expedition arrived before Pondicherry in July, and the siege was commenced in the beginning of August: the fortress capitulated on the 22nd of August.

A circumstance that occurred after the capture has

1793 been often since narrated by old officers of the corps, and, although in itself of a trivial nature, it may deserve to be recorded, as showing the good effect that it is possible to produce, even upon prejudiced enemies, by courtesy and firmness.

The SEVENTY-FOURTH formed part of the garrison, and the French troops remained in the place as prisoners of war. Their officers were of the old *régime,* and were gentlemen by birth and in manners, to whom it was incumbent to show every kindness and hospitality. It was found, however, that both officers and men, and the French population generally, were strongly tinctured with the revolutionary mania; and some uneasiness was felt lest the same should be in any degree imbibed by the British soldiers. It happened that the officers of the SEVENTY-FOURTH were in the theatre when a French officer called for the revolutionary air, "*Ca Ira;*" this was opposed by some of the British, and there was every appearance of a serious disturbance, both parties being highly excited. The SEVENTY-FOURTH, being in a body, had an opportunity to consult, and to act with effect; and, having taken their resolution, two or three of them made their way to the orchestra, the rest taking post at the doors, and, having obtained silence, the senior officer addressed the house in a firm but conciliatory manner. He stated that the national tune called for by one of the company ought not to be objected to, and that, as an act of courtesy to the ladies and others who had seconded the request, he and his brother officers were determined to support it with every mark of respect, and called upon their countrymen to do the same. It was accordingly played with the most uproarious applause on the part of the French, the British officers standing up uncovered;

but the moment it was finished, the house was called 1793
upon by the same party again to uncover to the British national air, "God save the King." They now appealed to the French, reminding them that each had their national attachments and recollections of home; that love of country was an honourable principle, and should be respected in each other; and that they felt assured their respected friends would not be behind in that courtesy which had just been shown by the British. Bravo! Bravo! resounded from every part of the house, and from that moment all rankling was at an end. They lived in perfect harmony till the French embarked; and each party retained their sentiments as a thing peculiar to their own country, but without the slightest offence on either side, or expectation that they should assimilate, more than if they related to the colour of their uniforms.

The regiment was deprived of the able services of 1794
Lieut.-Colonel Hamilton Maxwell, by his premature death at Cudalore on the 8th June, 1794. This officer had been at an early age appointed to a company of Fraser's Highlanders, in which corps he served during the whole of the American war with a degree of approbation which his later conduct, while in command of the SEVENTY-FOURTH, proved that he so well merited.

In the year 1797 the regiment was embarked for an 1797
expedition intended against *Manilla*, but was detained in consequence of the threatened renewal of hostilities in *Mysore*.

In October, 1797, the seventy-first regiment being ordered home from India, the SEVENTY-FOURTH was completed by two hundred men transferred from that corps.

In the year 1798, when voluntary contributions for 1798

1798 the support of the war with France were being offered to Government from various parts of the British dominions, the private men of each company of the SEVENTY-FOURTH sent a message to the officers commanding companies, saying that "in the present critical "exigency, when their country was threatened with an "invasion, they were sensible that it was the duty of "every Briton to strain every nerve, and exert every "power, to repel their inveterate enemies, the French, "and arrest the progress of their detestable principles; "they therefore had unanimously resolved to subscribe "eight days' pay to carry on the present war,—a war "unprovoked on our part, and justified by the noblest "of motives, the preservation of our invaluable con-"stitution."

The serjeants and corporals, animated by similar sentiments, subscribed half a month's pay each, and the officers added one month's pay.

1799 An army having been assembled at Vellore, by order of the Earl of Mornington (afterwards the Marquis Wellesley), Governor-General of India, under the command of Lieut.-General Harris, for the invasion of *Mysore*, the SEVENTY-FOURTH, with the twelfth and ninety-fourth, or Scots brigade, formed the first European brigade, under Major-General Baird, Major-General Bridges commanding the right wing of the army.

The army advanced on the 11th of February, 1799, and entered the Mysore territory on the 5th of March; but only reached Mallavelly on the 27th of March, when, on approaching the ground of encampment, the army of Tippoo Sultan was discovered drawn up on a height at a few miles distance. The advanced piquets were attacked by the enemy, and the whole wing advancing, a general action ensued. The enemy lost one thousand killed and wounded, and immediately retreated upon Seringapatam. 1799

The regiment was actively engaged, and repulsed a formidable attack of the enemy's cavalry on the right of the British line. The loss sustained by the victors was very small. The casualties of the regiment on this occasion were—

Killed	0	Officers	5	Non-commissioned officers and men	
Wounded	1	,,	17	,,	,,

Officer Wounded.
Lieutenant Moore.

The army advanced on the following day, and arrived before Seringapatam on the 5th of April. The preparations for the siege immediately commenced, and a breach being reported practicable on the 3rd of May, the assault was ordered for the following day, the 4th May, when it took place accordingly. The troops for the assault, commanded by Major-General Baird, were divided into two columns of attack. The SEVENTY-FOURTH, with the seventy-third regiment, 4 European flank companies, 14 Sepoy flank companies, with 50 artillerymen, formed the right column, under Colonel Sherbroke. Each column was preceded by one serjeant and twelve men, volunteers, supported by an advanced party of one subaltern, and twenty-five men. Lieutenant Hill, of the SEVENTY-FOURTH, commanded the advanced party of the right column. After the successful storm and capture of the fortress, the SEVENTY-FOURTH was the first regiment that entered the palace.

In the following order issued, on the 5th of May, by Lieut.-General Harris, the conduct of the regiment,

1799 and of Lieut.-Colonel Campbell, who commanded it on this occasion, was conspicuously noticed :—

"*Head Quarters, Camp before Seringapatam,*
5th May, 1799.

"GENERAL ORDER.

"The Commander-in-Chief congratulates the gal-"lant army, which he has the honour to command, on "the conquest of yesterday. The effects arising from "the attainment of such an acquisition as far exceed "the present limits of detail, as the unremitting zeal, "labour, and unparalleled valour of the troops surpass "power of praise for services so incalculable in their "consequences; he must consider the army as well "entitled to the applause and gratitude of their "country.

"On referring to the progress of the siege, so many "occasions have occurred for applause to the troops "employed that it is difficult to particularize indivi-"dual merit: but the gallant manner in which Lieut.-"Colonel Shaw, the Honorable Colonel Wellesley, "Lieut.-Colonel Moneypenny, the Honorable Lieut.-"Colonel St. John, Major McDonald, Major Skelly, and "Lieut.-Colonel Wallace, of the SEVENTY-FOURTH, "conducted the attacks entrusted to their guidance, in "the several outworks and posts of the enemy, demands "to be recorded, and the very spirited attack led by "Lieut.-Colonel Campbell* of His Majesty's SEVENTY-"FOURTH Regiment, which tended so greatly to secure "the position our troops had attained in the enemy's "works on the 26th ultimo, claims the strongest ap-"probation of the Commander-in-Chief."

---

* See Appendix No. 2, page 125.

The casualties of the regiment during the siege were :— 1799

Killed	5 Officers	45	Non-commissioned officers and men
Wounded	4 ,,	111	,, ,,

Officers Killed.	*Officers Wounded.*
Lieutenant Irvine	Lieutenant Fletcher
,, Farquhar	,, Aytone
,, Hill	,, Maxwell
,, Shaw	,, Carrington
,, Prendergast	

The regiment has received the Royal authority to bear the word "SERINGAPATAM" on its regimental colour and appointments in commemoration of its services at this siege.

On the breaking up of the army in September, 1799, the regiment returned to Bangalore; being afterwards ordered back to Madras, it was halted at Wallajahbad in the beginning of 1800, when the flank 1800 companies were employed at the siege and capture of the Fort of Pandellumcourchy, and the regiment was engaged in various operations against the Southern Polygars, during which great exertions were made and losses sustained, of which no distinct record has been preserved.

In the spring of 1801, six companies were sent to 1801 Bombay, to replace troops withdrawn for the expedition to Egypt. On the 4th of June in that year, the anniversary of His Majesty's birth-day, when the Imperial Union flag was hoisted for the first time at Bombay, a *feu-de-joie* was fired by the detachments of the SEVENTY-FOURTH, eighty-sixth, and eighty-eighth regiments.

The regiment formed part of the force assembled 1802 under Lieut.-General Stuart at Hurryhur, on the north-western frontier of Mysore, in the month of November, 1802, by order of Lord Clive.

In consequence of instructions from the Governor-

1802 General the Marquis Wellesley, Lieut. General Stuart formed a detachment from the main army to advance into the Mahratta States, under Major-General the Honourable Arthur Wellesley. This force consisted of the nineteenth dragoons, SEVENTY-FOURTH, and ninety-fourth (Scots Brigade) King's regiments, (the ninety-fourth afterwards joined Colonel Stevenson's detach-
1803 ment on the 16th of April, 1803); three regiments of native cavalry, and six battalions of native infantry, with a proportion of artillery. The force commenced its advance on the 9th of March, 1803.

The cavalry and advanced guard arrived at Poonah on the 20th, and the main body on the 22nd of April; here every exertion was made to refit and get into a state of efficiency for the active campaign that was to follow.

The zealous and soldier-like feeling, which pervaded all ranks of the SEVENTY-FOURTH, was exemplified by the conduct of the officers of the regiment upon this occasion: all of them being distressed as to the completion of their camp equipage, having lost upon the long march, through a variety of country, two sets of cattle, and now requiring a third, besides other supplies which their exhausted means could not furnish. A petition was got up by the officers of one of the regiments, setting forth their hardships, and praying for aid on account of past losses and present wants. It was actually signed and carried to the lines of another regiment, with a view of obtaining, in succession, the signatures of the whole European part of the force. The moment the SEVENTY-FOURTH heard of it, a deputation of their officers went to the regiment where it had originated, and strongly remonstrated upon the impropriety of the measure. They stated their own

unanimous determination to submit to any loss, and 1803
bear every hardship which the service might require, trusting to the generosity of the Government after the service should be performed; and asking what confidence the General could have in his troops, if they should beset him with such an application near an enemy, and when he must be engrossed with the public departments: these arguments prevailed, and the petition was abandoned.

The force advanced from Poonah on the 26th of April, and the regiment was actively engaged throughout the whole of the following brilliant campaign; at the capture of the town and fort of Ahmednuggur, on the 8th and 12th August, its conduct was particularly noticed in Major-General Wellesley's despatch. The following General Orders were published by him, and by the Governor-General on the occasion:—

" *Camp at Ahmednuggur, 12th August,* 1803.

" GENERAL ORDER.

" Major-General Wellesley congratulates the troops " upon the result of the operations carried on against " the fort of *Ahmednuggur*. His thanks are particularly " due to the troops who made the brisk and gallant " attack upon the city, upon the 8th inst., and to Lieut.- " Colonels Harness, Wallace (of the SEVENTY-FOURTH), " and Maxwell, commanding brigades, and to Captain " Beauman of artillery, Captain Johnston of engineers, " and Captain Heitland of pioneers.

" A royal salute to be fired immediately upon the " taking possession of the fort of Ahmednuggur, and, " upon the receipt of this order, in all the garrisons and " detachments of troops under the command of Major- " General Wellesley in the territories of the Company,

1803 "the Rajah of Mysore, His Highness the Nizam, and "the Mahrattas."

GENERAL ORDER BY THE GOVERNOR-GENERAL.

"*Fort William*, 8*th September*, 1803.

"The Governor-General in Council having received "from Major-General the Hon. Arthur Wellesley the "official account of the reduction of the important "fortress of *Ahmednuggur*, by the forces under the "command of that officer, is pleased to signify the high "approbation with which his Excellency in Council has "observed the judgment, promptitude, and skill, mani-"fested by Major-General the Hon. Arthur Wellesley, "in directing the operations of the forces under his "command on that critical occasion.

"His Excellency in Council is pleased to direct Major-"General the Hon. Arthur Wellesley to notify to the "troops under his command, that the Governor-General "in Council has derived the most cordial satisfaction "from the distinguished alacrity, gallantry, and spirit, "which they displayed in their attack upon the pettah, "and in the subsequent siege of the fort of Ahmed-"nuggur; and the Governor-General in Council has "remarked with particular approbation the conduct of "Lieut.-Colonels Harness, Wallace (of the SEVENTY-"FOURTH), and Maxwell, of Captain Beauman of artil-"lery, of Captain Johnston of engineers, and of Captain "Heitland of the pioneers.

"The Governor-General in Council deeply laments "the loss of Captains Grant and Humberstone, Lieu-"tenants Anderson and Plenderleath, and of the brave "soldiers who fell in the successful contest of the 8th "August.

"The memory of these gallant officers and soldiers, "who have fallen with honour in the public service, will

" be regarded with affection and respect by their Sove- 1803
" reign and their country."

On the 23rd of September, Major-General the Hon. Arthur Wellesley attacked the whole combined Mahratta army of Scindiah, and the Rajah of Berar, at *Assaye,* on the banks of the Kaitna river, when the Mahratta force of 40,000 men was completely defeated by a force of 5000, of which not more than 2000 were Europeans, losing 98 pieces of cannon, 7 standards, and leaving 1200 killed, and about four times that number wounded on the field. The conduct of the SEVENTY-FOURTH, in this memorable battle, was most gallant and distinguished, but from having been prematurely led against the village of Assaye, on the left of the enemy's line, the regiment was exposed, unsupported, to a most terrible cannonade, and being afterwards charged by cavalry, sutained a tremendous loss.

The casualties in the regiment on this occasion were—

Killed	11 Officers,	9 Serjeants,	0 Drummers,	104 Rank and File.
Wounded	6 ,,	17 ,,	4 ,,	250 ,,

Officers Killed.	*Officers Wounded.*
Captain D. Aytone.	Major Swinton.
,, Andrew Dyce.	Capt. and Lieut. Moore.
,, Roderick McLeod.	Lieutenant Mein.
,, John Maxwell.	,, McMurdo.
Lieut. John Campbell.	,, Shawe.
,, John Morshead Campbell.	Ensign Kearnan.
,, Lorn Campbell.	
,, James Grant.	
,, J. Morris.	
,, Robert Neilson.	
,, Volunteer Tew.	

Every officer present with the regiment was either killed or wounded, except Quarter-master James Grant, who when he saw so many of his friends fall in

1803 the battle, resolved to share their fate, and though a non combatant, joined the ranks and fought to the termination of the action.

The regiment was marched off the field by Major Swinton (although wounded), and Quarter master Grant, every other officer having been disabled.

Major-General Wellesley stated, in his despatch to the Governor-General, of the 24th September :—

" I cannot write in too strong terms of the conduct " of the troops; they advanced in the best order, and " with the greatest steadiness, under a most destructive " fire, against a body of infantry far superior in number, " who appeared determined to contend with them to " the last, and who were driven from their guns only " by the bayonet; and notwithstanding the numbers of " the enemy's cavalry, and the repeated demonstrations " they made of an intention to charge, they were kept " at a distance by our infantry.

" I am particularly indebted to Lieutenant-Colonel " Harness and Lieutenant-Colonel Wallace, of the " SEVENTY-FOURTH, for the manner in which they con- " ducted their brigades."

And in his memorandum on the battle he added :—

" However, by one of those unlucky accidents which " frequently happen, the officer commanding the " piquets which were upon the right, led immediately " up to the village of Assaye. The SEVENTY-FOURTH " regiment, which was on the right of the second line, " and was ordered to support the piquets, followed " them. There was a large break in our line between " these corps and those on our left. They were exposed " to a most terrible cannonade from Assaye, and were " charged by the cavalry belonging to the Campoos;

"consequently in the piquets and the SEVENTY-FOURTH 1803
"regiment, we sustained the greatest part of our
"loss.

"Another bad consequence resulting from this "mistake, was the necessity of introducing the cavalry "into the action at too early a period. I had ordered "it to watch the motions of the enemy's cavalry hanging "upon our right, and luckily it charged in time to save "the remains of the SEVENTY-FOURTH and the piquets."

Also in a letter of 3rd of October:—

"Our loss is great, but the action I believe was the "most severe that ever was fought in this country, and "I believe such a quantity of cannon and such advan-"tages have seldom been gained, by any single victory, "in any part of the world."

The following General Orders were published on the occasion:—

GENERAL ORDER BY MAJOR-GENERAL WELLESLEY.

"*Camp near Assaye,*
Saturday, 24*th September*, 1803.

"Major-General Wellesley returns his thanks to the "troops for their conduct in the action of yesterday, the "result of which is so honorable to them, and likely to "be so advantageous to the public interests. He re-"quests Lieutenant-Colonel Harness and Lieutenant-"Colonel Wallace (of the SEVENTY-FOURTH regiment) "in particular will accept his acknowledgments for "the manner in which they conducted their respective "brigades.

"A royal salute to be fired in camp this afternoon, "upon the occasion of the victory gained over the "enemy's army yesterday; and a royal salute to be "fired on the same occasion on receipt of this order in

1803 "each of the detachments, and in each of the garrisons "under the command of Major-General Wellesley in "the territories of the Company, of the Soubah, of the "Deccan, of the Peshwah, and of the Rajah Anund Rao "Guickwar."

GENERAL ORDER BY THE GOVERNOR-GENERAL.

"*Fort William*, 30*th October*, 1803.

"The Governor-General in Council has this day re-"ceived from Major-General the Honorable Arthur "Wellesley the official report of the signal and splendid "victory obtained by the troops under the personal "command of that distinguished officer on the 23rd of "September, at Assaye, in the Deccan, over the com-"bined armies of Dowlut Rao Scindiah, and the Rajah "of Berar.

"At the close of a campaign of the most brilliant "success and glory in every quarter of India, this "transcendant victory demands a testimony of public "honor, equal to any which the justice of the British "Government in India has ever conferred on the con-"duct of our officers and troops in the most distinguished "period of our military history.

"The Governor-General in Council highly approves "of the skilful plan formed by Major-General the "Honorable Arthur Wellesley on the 21st September, "for precluding the escape of the enemy, and for re-"ducing their combined army to the necessity of "hazarding a general action. His Excellency in Council "also signifies his most cordial approbation of the "magnanimity, promptitude, and judgment with which "Major-General the Honorable Arthur Wellesley de-"termined upon the instantaneous attack of the enemy "on the 23rd September. During the severe action "which ensued, the conduct of Major-General the

" Honorable Arthur Wellesley united a degree of 1803
" ability, of prudence, and of dauntless spirit, seldom
" equalled, and never surpassed.

" The Governor-General in Council signifies his " warmest applause of the exemplary order and steadi- " ness with which the troops advanced under a most " destructive fire, against a body of the enemy's infantry " considerably superior in number, and determined to " oppose a vigorous resistance to our attack. The " numerous infantry of the enemy were driven from their " powerful artillery, at the point of the bayonet, with an " alacrity and resolution truly worthy of British soldiers, " and the firmness and discipline manifested by our " brave infantry, in repelling the great body of the " enemy's cavalry, merit the highest commendation.

"The Governor-General in Council has remarked " with great satisfaction the gallant and skilful conduct " of the cavalry commanded by Lieutenant-Colonel " Maxwell, and particularly of His Majesty's nineteenth " regiment of light dragoons, a corps distinguished by " a long and uninterrupted course of arduous service, " and of progressive honor.

" His Excellency in Council directs Major-General the " Honorable Arthur Wellesley to signify to all the officers " and troops employed on this glorious occasion, and " especially to Lieutenant-Colonel Harness and Lieu- " tenant-Colonel Wallace, SEVENTY-FOURTH regiment, " who commanded brigades, and to the Officers of the " Staff, the high sense entertained by the Governor- " General in Council of their eminent and honorable " services.

" The important benefits arising from the triumph " of our arms in the battle of Assaye are not inferior to " the splendour of the action. The immediate con-

1803 "'sequences derived from the exertions of that day, have "been the complete defeat of the combined army of the "confederate chieftains, an irreparable blow to the "strength and efficiency of their military resources, "especially of their artillery in the Deccan, the expul-"sion of a hostile and predatory army from the territory "of our ally the Soubahdar of the Deccan, and a "seasonable and effectual check to the ambition, pride, "and rapacity of the enemy.

"The prosperous result of these advantages must be "accelerated by the auspicious progress of our arms in "other provinces of India, and it may reasonably be "expected that the decisive victories gained at Delhi "and Assaye, on the 11th and 23rd of September, will "speedily compel the enemy to restore peace to Hin-"doostan, and to the Deccan.

"The achievements of our commanders, officers, and "troops during this campaign, and especially in the "signal victories of Delhi, and of Assaye, must "inspire a general sentiment of just confidence in the "vigor of our military resources, and in the stability of "our dominion and power. Our uniform success in "frustrating every advantage of superior numbers, of "powerful artillery, and even of obstinate resistance "opposed by the enemy, constitutes a satisfactory proof "of the established superiority of British discipline, "experience, and valor; and demonstrates that the "glorious progress of our arms is not the accidental "result of a temporary or transient advantage, but the "natural and certain effect of a permanent cause.

"From these reflections, consolation is to be derived "for the loss of those lamented and honored officers and "soldiers, who, animated by the gallant spirit of their "General, and emulating the noble example of his zeal

"and courage, sacrificed their lives to the honor and 1803
"interests of their country.

"The Governor-General in Council greatly regrets the "loss of Lieutenant-Colonel Maxwell, of His Majesty's "nineteenth dragoons, who fell at the head of the "British cavalry, bravely charging a large body of the "enemy's infantry. With the utmost concern his "Excellency in Council records the names of the valuable "and excellent officers who have fallen with glory at the "battle of Assaye, in achieving the complete defeat of "the enemy, and in establishing the triumph of the "British arms in the Deccan; Lieutenant-Colonel "Maxwell, Captains R. Boyle, H. Mackay, D. Aytone, "A. Dyce, R. Macleod, and T. Maxwell, Captain-Lieu-"tenants Steel and Fowler, Lieutenants Bonomi, "Griffith, J. Campbell, J. M. Campbell, J. Grant, R. "Neilson, L. Campbell, M. Morris, and J. Douglas, "Brown, Mavor, Perrie, and Volunteer Tew.*

"In testimony of the high honor acquired by the army "under the personal command of Major-General the "Honorable A. Wellesley, at the battle of Assaye, the "Governor-General in Council is pleased to order that "honorary Colours, with a device properly suited to com-"memorate that signal and splendid victory, be pre-"sented to the corps of cavalry and infantry employed "on that glorious occasion.

"The names of the brave officers and men who fell "at the battle of Assaye will be commemorated, to-"gether with the circumstances of the action, upon the "public monument to be erected at Fort William, to "the memory of those who have fallen in the public "service, during the present campaign. The honorary

* Mr. Tew had been recommended by Major-General Wellesley to the Commander-in-Chief for his conduct at Ahmednuggur.

1803 "Colours granted by these orders to His Majesty's "nineteenth regiment of dragoons, and to the SEVENTY-"FOURTH and seventy-eighth regiments of foot, are "to be used by these corps, while they shall con-"tinue in India, or until His Majesty's most gracious "pleasure be signified through his Excellency the "Commander-in-Chief.

"His Excellency the most noble the Governor-Gene-"ral, Captain General, and Commander-in-Chief of "all the land forces serving in the East Indies, is "pleased to direct, that these orders be publicly read "to the troops under arms at every station of the land "forces in the East Indies, and that the European "officers of native corps do cause the same to be ex-"plained to the native officers and troops.

"By command of his Excellency the most noble the "Governor-General in Council.

(Signed) "L. HOOK,
"*Secretary to the Government*
Military Department."

The regiment has received the Royal authority to bear on the regimental Colour and Appointments the "Elephant," with the word "ASSAYE" superscribed, in commemoration of the gallantry and good conduct displayed by the corps in the battle fought at *Assaye* on the 23rd of September, 1803.

After the battle of Assaye, the SEVENTY-FOURTH was struck off duty on account of its severe losses, while Major-General Wellesley remained with his force in the same district of country; but on the 25th of October he recommenced a series of active movements in pursuit of the Rajah of Berar, and on the 29th of November, having been joined by the subsidiary force under Colonel Stevenson, he attacked and completely de-

feated the united armies of Scindiah and the Rajah of 1803
Berar on the plains of Argaum.

General Wellesley, in his despatch to the Governor-General, dated Camp, Parterly, 30th November, 1803, stated,—

"The troops had marched a great distance on a very "hot day, and I therefore did not think it proper to "pursue them (the enemy), but, shortly after our "arrival here, bodies of horse appeared in our front, "with which the Mysore cavalry skirmished during a "part of the day, and when I went out to push for-"ward the piquets of the infantry to support the "Mysore cavalry, and to take up the ground of our "encampment, I could perceive distinctly a long line "of infantry, cavalry, and artillery, regularly drawn "up on the plains of Argaum, immediately in front of "that village, and about six miles from this place, at "which I intended to encamp.

"Although late in the day, I immediately determined "to attack this army. Accordingly I marched on in "one column, the British cavalry leading in a direction "nearly parallel to that of the enemy's line; covering "the rear and left by the Mogul and Mysore cavalry. "The enemy's infantry and guns were in the left of "their centre, with a body of cavalry on their left. "Scindiah's army, consisting of one very heavy body of "cavalry, was on the right, having upon its right a body "of Pindarries and other light troops. Their line ex-"tended above five miles, having in their rear the vil-"lage and extensive gardens and enclosures of Argaum; "and in their front a plain, which, however, was much "cut by water-courses, &c. I formed the army in two "lines; the infantry in the first, the cavalry in the "second, and supporting the right; and the Mogul and

1803 "Mysore cavalry the left, nearly parallel to that of "the enemy; with the right rather advanced, in order "to press upon the enemy's left. Some time clapsed "before the lines could be formed, owing to a part of "the infantry of my division, which led the column, "having got into some confusion.

"When formed, the whole advanced in the greatest "order, the SEVENTY-FOURTH and seventy-eighth regi-"ments were attacked by a large body (supposed to "be Persians), and all these were destroyed. Scindiah's "cavalry charged the first battalion sixth regiment, "which was on the left of our line, and were repulsed; "and their whole line retired in disorder before our "troops, leaving in our hands thirty-eight pieces of "cannon and all their ammunition.

"The British cavalry then pursued them for several "miles, destroyed great numbers, and took many ele-"phants and camels, and much baggage.

"The troops conducted themselves with their usual "bravery. The SEVENTY-FOURTH and seventy-eighth "regiments had a particular opportunity of distinguish-"ing themselves, and have deserved and received my "thanks."

Major-General Wellesley said in another letter of 2nd December:—"If we had had daylight one hour "more, not a man would have escaped.

"The troops were under arms, and I was on horse-"back from six in the morning until twelve at night."

The following General Order was issued:—

"*Camp, near the Plains of Argaum,*
Wednesday, 30*th Nov.*, 1803.

"Major-General Wellesley congratulates the troops "upon the success of yesterday, which he has every

" reason to hope was effected without great loss. The 1803
" Major-General's thanks are due upon this occasion to " all the troops, for the perseverance with which they " went through the fatigues of the day, and for the " steadiness they displayed during the action, but in " particular the SEVENTY FOURTH and seventy-eighth " regiments.

" To Colonel Stevenson for the advice and assist-" ance he received from him, to Lieutenant-Colonel " Wallace, SEVENTY-FOURTH regiment, &c."

The casualties in the regiment on the occasion were :—

	Officers.	Sergeants.	Drummers.	Rank and File.
Killed	0	1	0	3
Wounded	1	5	1	41

Officer Wounded.

Lieutenant Langlands.

After the battle of Argaum, General Wellesley (as he stated in his despatch of the 15th December to the Governor-General) determined to lose no time in commencing the siege of *Gawilghur*, a very strong fort, situated on a range of mountains between the sources of the rivers Poorna and Taptee: he accordingly marched on, and arrived with both divisions at Ellichpoor on the 5th December, whence, after establishing an hospital for the men wounded at Argaum, both divisions advanced to Gawilghur on the 7th December. After a long series of laborious services, which were chiefly performed by Colonel Stevenson's division, the batteries opened on the 13th December, and the breach of the outer fort being reported practicable on the following night, the storm took place on the 15th December.

1803 The following Order was issued on the occasion:—

"*Camp, Deogaum, Thursday*, 15 *Dec.*, 1803.

"GENERAL ORDER.

"Major-General Wellesley has great satisfaction in "congratulating the troops under his command upon "the brilliant success of this day.

"In the course of this short but active and laborious "siege, Major-General Wellesley has, with pleasure, "observed in all a most anxious and zealous desire to "forward the service, the most steady perseverance in "the performance of laborious services, which would be "thought impracticable by other troops, and that gal-"lantry, when opposed to the enemy, which they have "shown so frequently during the campaign, and which "has carried them with honour through so many diffi-"culties.

"Although the brilliant part of the service did not "fall to the lot of the division under his immediate "command, Major-General Wellesley observed, with "satisfaction, the exertions they made in the part "allotted to them; and his thanks are particularly due "to Captain Beauman, commanding the artillery, and "to Lieutenant-Colonels Wallace (of the SEVENTY-"FOURTH) and Chalmers, for the manner in which they "conducted the attacks respectively entrusted to their "commands."

In a letter to General Lake, Commander-in-Chief in India, of the 5th January, Major-General Wellesley stated:—"On the 15th of December I took the hill "fort of Gawilghur by storm; on the 19th I signed a "peace with the Rajah of Berar; and on the 30th "December one with Scindiah.

"I must again take the liberty of mentioning to you "Lieutenant-Colonel Wallace of the SEVENTY-FOURTH

" regiment, whose services I have again had occasion 1803
" to report in a favourable manner, since I addressed
" you upon the subject after the battle of Assaye."

After the conclusion of the peace, the troops under 1804
General Wellesley were gradually drawn off to the westward and southward, and being at Neemgaum on the 2nd of February, 1804, the SEVENTY-FOURTH regiment was selected by Major-General Wellesley, with the first battalion eighth native infantry, one hundred and fifty pioneers, and one hundred men from each battalion of native infantry, all the cavalry of the division, two six-pounders, and two brass twelve-pounders, to march on the following morning, under his own command, in pursuit of bands of freebooters, who had infested the neighbourhood, but had retired upon Perinda, the remainder of the division being left under the command of Lieutenant-Colonel Wallace at Neemgaum. Major Swinton of the SEVENTY-FOURTH commanded the infantry of the expedition.

Major-General Wellesley said, in a letter to Lieut.-General Stewart, dated, Camp at Munkaiseer, 7th February, 1804:—

" I left my camp on the 3rd, about thirty miles south-
" east from Ahmednuggur, and I arrived by forced
" marches at Sailgaon, near Perinda, on the 4th. I there
" heard that the enemy were at this place, twenty-four
" miles from me, and although I had marched twenty
" miles that morning, I determined to march on in the
" night. The road was very bad, and till one o'clock
" the night was very dark, and we made but little pro-
" gress. The consequence was, that we did not arrive
" till nine in the morning, instead of at daylight. The
" enemy had received intelligence of my approach; I
" believe from my own camp. They had struck their

1804 "camp and had begun their march, but were still in "sight. I pursued them with the cavalry, cut up "some, and took all their guns, baggage, bazaar, &c., "and followed them as long as they remained collected. "I had with me the cavalry, the SEVENTY-FOURTH "regiment, the first of the eighth, and five hundred "men from other regiments."

In a General Order, dated "Monday the 6th of February, 1804," this service is thus alluded to:—

"Major-General Wellesley thanks the troops for the "persevering activity with which they underwent the "fatigues of the march on the 4th and 5th instant. The "advance of the infantry under Major Swinton was "very proper, and in the best order.

"The detachment will halt to-morrow."

In a letter of the 7th February, Major-General Wellesley added:—

"The exertion made by the troops is the greatest "I ever witnessed. Everything was over by twelve "o'clock on the 5th, and I think that by that time the "infantry must have marched 60 miles, from six in the "morning of the 4th. We halted from twelve in the "day till ten at night on the 4th, so that we marched "sixty miles, with infantry, in twenty hours."

On this expedition, the infantry arrived at the point of attack at the same time with the cavalry; it has often since been remarked by the Duke of Wellington as the greatest march he ever made.

Major-General Wellesley left his army near Perinda, on the 24th of February, under the command of Lieut.-Colonel Wallace; he returned to it in the end of May, but at Poonah, on the 24th of June, 1804, he finally gave up the command, leaving the SEVENTY-FOURTH as part of the subsidiary force serving with the Peshwah, under Lieut.-Colonal Wallace, who had been promoted 1804 from a majority in the SEVENTY-FOURTH to the Lieutenant-Colonelcy of the 19th Dragoons, at the recommendation of General Wellesley, in consequence of his distinguished services at the battle of Assaye, and in succession to Lieut.-Colonel Maxwell, who was killed in that action.

The following General Order was issued by Major-General the Hon. Arthur Wellesley :—

"*Camp at Poonah, Sunday, 24th June*, 1804.

"GENERAL ORDER.

"The following corps, &c., are to compose the sub-"sidiary force serving with His Highness the Peshwah, "under command of Lieut.-Colonel Wallace.

"5th and 7th regiments native cavalry.

"Detachments of Madras, and Bombay artillery.

"His Majesty's SEVENTY-FOURTH and 78th regiments.

"1st battalion, 2nd regiment, Madras native infantry.

"2nd battalion, 3rd ,, ,,

"1st battalion, 8th ,, ,,

"2nd battalion, 18th ,, ,,

"Upon the occasion of quitting the army, in conse-"quence of the orders of the Governor-General, Major-"General Wellesley once more returns his thanks to "the officers and troops, for their uniform good conduct "since he has had the honour of commanding them. "In the space of little more than a year, those in this "quarter in particular, now composing the subsidiary "forces serving with the Peshwah and the Soubahdar "of the Deccan, and those which are under orders to "march to the southward, have been tried in every "mode in which it is possible to try troops, and have.

1804 "uniformily manifested that patience under fatigues "and severity of climate, that activity and perseverance "in labour, and bravery and discipline in action, which "are the characteristic qualities of the best soldiers; "their success and the honour which the troops have "acquired, are proportionate to the good qualities "which they have displayed; on which qualities Major-"General Wellesley has always had the fullest reliance "in every emergency of the service. He now recom-"mends to them an adherence to the principles which "have brought them with honour through so many "difficulties, as the certain pledge of future success.

"Major-General Wellesley has frequently reported "the good conduct of the troops to the Commander-in-"Chief and the Governor-General, and has recom-"mended them to the notice of their Excellencies. He "will not fail to recommend individuals, who have had "opportunities of distinguishing themselves, whenever "an occasion may offer, and he assures all, that he shall "ever remember and reflect with satisfaction on their "conduct and services, and that in every situation in "which he may be placed, he shall be happy to forward "their views."

In the month of August (a rupture with Holkar having been some time commenced,) Lieut.-Colonel Wallace and his division left Poonah, on march towards his country, and on the 8th of October reached Chandore, a strong hill fort in Candeish, which surrendered on the 12th of October; they marched again on the 17th, and on the 21st of October reached Gaulnah, another hill fort, which surrendered after two days' battering. Such was the temper of the corps, that when upon this occasion, for the last time in India, a call was made upon it for a forlorn hope, the whole regiment turned out at once. The place was surrendered, but it was an ugly and imperfect breach, and had it been stormed, the party must have been drawn by lot. 1804

On the 3rd of November the division quitted Gaulnah, leaving a small garrison.

On the 8th of May, 1805, the division was at Ahmednuggur, left it on the 24th, taking a northern direction, and arrived at Palud, forty miles beyond Aurungabad, on the 10th of June, when Lieut.-Colonel Wallace having received orders to send back to Ahmednuggur the troops belonging to the Madras Presidency, the SEVENTY-FOURTH marched accordingly with the first, fifth, and seventh regiments of native cavalry, and six guns, under command of Lieut.-Colonel Huddlestone, of the Company's service, and arrived at Ahmednuggur on the 24th of June. 1805

The regiment embarked at Bombay, and landed at Madras in July, 1805.

The SEVENTY-FOURTH HIGHLANDERS having now served for sixteen years in the East Indies, during which they had been almost continually in the field, and acquired a character of unparalleled excellence for gallantry and good conduct, the small but gallant remnant of their many arduous campaigns was ordered to return to Europe.

The following Order in Council was issued on the occasion by the Governor, Lord William Bentinck.

"*Fort St. George,*
5th September, 1805.

"The Right Honorable the Governor in Council, "on the intended embarkation of the remaining officers "and men of His Majesty's SEVENTY-FOURTH regi- "ment, discharges a duty of the highest satisfaction to "his Lordship in Council, in bestowing on that dis-

1805 " tinguished corps a public testimony of his Lordship's " warmest respect and approbation. During a long " and eventful period of residence in India, the con- " duct of His Majesty's SEVENTY-FOURTH regiment, " whether in peace or war, has been equally exemplary " and conspicuous, having been not less remarkable for " the general tenor of its discipline, than for the most " glorious achievements in the field.

" Impressed with these sentiments, his Lordship in " Council is pleased to direct, that His Majesty's " SEVENTY-FOURTH regiment be held forth as an object " of imitation for the military establishment of this " Presidency, as his Lordship will ever reflect with " pride and gratification, that in the Actions, which have " led to the present pre-eminence of the British Empire " in India, the part so nobly sustained by that corps will " add lustre to the military annals of the country, and " crown the name of His Majesty's SEVENTY-FOURTH " regiment with immortal reputation.

" It having been ascertained, to the satisfaction of the " Governor in Council, that the Officers of His Majesty's " SEVENTY-FOURTH regiment were, during the late " campaign in the Deccan, subjected to extraordinary " expenses, which have been aggravated by the arrange- " ments connected with their embarkation for Europe, " his Lordship in Council has been pleased to resolve, " that those officers shall receive a gratuity equal to " three months' batta, as a further testimony of his " Lordship's approbation of their eminent services.

" By order of the Right Honorable the Governor in Council.

(Signed) " J. H. WEBB.

" *Secretary to the Government.*"

Although the history of the part borne by the

SEVENTY-FOURTH HIGHLANDERS in the more conspi- 1805
cuous and generally known operations of warfare, from the period of their formation until they returned from India, as recorded in the Regimental Books, and other authentic official documents, is now completed; it remains to be noticed, that these greater operations formed a portion only of the continual conflicts and arduous services in which the regiment was engaged, (either as a corps, or by detachments,) of which no regular record has been preserved, but which contributed to raise its character to the exalted position it held in the opinion of the authorities, military and civil, of British India, testified by the public documents already inserted. Some details illustrative of these services, and of the system of discipline which was established in the regiment, have been communicated by Officers who served with it in India, and afterwards throughout the Peninsular War.

One of these officers (Captain Cargill*), stated, in a letter of the 22nd of December, 1830, to Lieut.-Colonel Mein, who then commanded the regiment, and whose personal knowledge of it extended over the same period:—

"The SEVENTY-FOURTH lives in my recollection under "two aspects, and during two distinct epochs. The first is "the history and character of the regiment, from its for- "mation to its return as a skeleton from India; and the

---

* Captain Cargill entered the army as Ensign in the eighty fourth regiment on the 21st of May, 1802, was, on the 23rd September, 1803, promoted to a Lieutenancy in the SEVENTY-FOURTH HIGHLANDERS, and, on the 31st December, 1812, to a company. He was present at the battles of Busaco, (where he was severely wounded), Vittoria, Pyrenees, Nivelle, Nive, Orthes, and Toulouse: he retired from the army on the 1st June, 1820, and has since received the War Medal, and Clasps, for his services.

1805 "second is that of the regiment as it now exists, from "its being embarked for the Peninsula in January, "1810.

"So far as field service is concerned, it has been the "good fortune of the corps to serve during both periods, "on the more conspicuous occasions, under the great "Captain of the age; under him also, during the latter "period, it received the impress of that character which "attaches to most regiments that were placed in the "same circumstances, which arose from the regulations "introduced by His Royal Highness the Duke of York, "and the practical application of them by a master "mind in the great school of the Peninsular War. Uni-"formity was thus given; and the SEVENTY-FOURTH, "like every other corps which has had the same train-"ing, must acknowledge the hand under which its "present character was mainly impressed. But it was "not so with the SEVENTY-FOURTH in India. At that "time every regiment had its distinctive character and "system broadly marked, and which was generally "found to have arisen from the materials of which it "had been originally composed, and the tact of the "officer by whom it had been embodied and trained. "The SEVENTY-FOURTH in these respects had been "fortunate, and the tone and discipline introduced by "the late Sir Archibald Campbell, together with the "chivalrous spirit and noble emulation imbibed by "the corps in these earlier days of eastern conquest, "had impressed upon the officers the most correct per-"ception of their duties, not only as regards internal "economy and the gradation of military rank, but "also as regards the Government under which they "served. It was, perhaps, the most perfect that could "well exist. It was participated in by the men, and

"certainly characterized the regiment in a strong 1805
"degree.

"It was an established principle in the old SEVENTY-"FOURTH, that whatever was required of the soldier, "should be strikingly set before him by his officers, "and hence the most minute point of ordinary duty "was regarded by the latter, as a matter in which his "honor was implicated. The duty of the officer of the "day was most rigidly attended to; the officer on duty "remaining in full uniform, and without parting with "his sword even in the hottest weather, and under all "circumstances, and frequently going the rounds of "the cantonments during the night. An exchange of "duty was almost never heard of, and the same system "was carried into every duty and department, with the "most advantageous effect upon the spirit and habits "of the men.

"Intemperance was an evil habit fostered by climate "and the great facility of indulgence; but it was a "point of honor among the men, never to indulge when "near an enemy, and I often heard it observed, that "this rule was never known to be broken, even under "the protracted operations of a siege. On such occasions "the officers had no trouble with it, the principle being "upheld by the men themselves.

"On one occasion, while the SEVENTY-FOURTH was in "garrison at Madras, and had received a route to march "up the country, there was a mutiny among the Com-"pany's artillery at the Mount. The evening before "the regiment set out it was reported that they had "some kind of leaning towards the mutineers; the "whole corps felt most indignant at the calumny, but "no notice was taken of it by the commanding officer. "In the morning, however, he marched early, and made

1805 "direct for the Mount, where he unfurled the colours, "and marched through the cantonments with fixed "bayonets. By a forced march he reached his proper "destination before midnight, and before dismissing "the men, he read them a short but pithy despatch, "which he sent off to the Government, stating the in- "dignation of every man of the corps at the libellous "rumour, and that he had taken the liberty of gratify- "ing his men, by showing to the mutineers those colours "which were ever faithfully devoted to the service of "the Government. The circumstance had also a happy "effect upon the mutineers who had heard the report, "but the stern aspect of the regiment dispelled the "illusion, and they submitted to their officers."

The losses sustained by the regiment in officers and men, on many occasions, of which no account has been kept, were very great, particularly during the last six years of its Indian service.

That gallant veteran Quarter-master Grant, who had been in the regiment from the time it was raised, fought at Assaye, and returned with it to England, used to say that he had seen nearly three different sets of officers during the period, the greater part of whom had fallen in battle or died of wounds, the regiment having been always very healthy.*

The memory of many individual acts of gallantry performed by officers and men has been lost, and before the SEVENTY-FOURTH left India, nearly all of the men who were fit for service, availed themselves of the privilege of volunteering for other regiments, to remain in a country to which they had become attached. One of these excellent soldiers, of the Grenadier Company, is

---

* See list of Officers who died during the service of the regiment in the East Indies, in Appendix No. 3, page 129.

mentioned as having volunteered on nine forlorn hopes, 1805
including Seringapatam.

The regiment embarked (a mere skeleton as to effective men,) at Madras on the 8th of September, 1805, and landed at Portsmouth on the 16th of February, 1806. 1806

Lieut.-Colonel Samuel Swinton returned to England in command of the regiment. He had been first appointed to it, as Lieutenant and Adjutant, on the 25th of December, 1787, and remained with it throughout its Indian service. He was promoted to a Majority on the 17th of May, 1800. As a Major he commanded the regiment during the campaigns of 1803 and 1804, (both the Lieut.-Colonels, Shaw and Campbell, being absent, and the other regimental Major, Lieut.-Colonel Wallace, being in command of a brigade.) He was severely wounded at Assaye. He had been promoted to the seventy-fifth regiment on the 13th of May, 1805, before his return to England.

The regiment has received the Royal authority to bear on its colours and appointments, the words "SERINGAPATAM" and "ASSAYE," in commemoration of its distinguished services at the capture of Seringapatam on the 4th of May, 1799, and at the battle of Assaye, on the 23rd of September, 1803; and also to bear a third colour for Assaye, conferred by the order of the Governor-General of India, as already mentioned, and presented to the regiment by the East India Company. In consequence, however, of the inconvenience caused by taking a third officer from his duty to carry this colour, it has been since ordered by the Commander-in-Chief to be discontinued in the field, and to be carried only "at reviews, inspections, and on gala days."*

* These orders were contained in a letter addressed to the Lieut.-General commanding the forces in Ireland, by the Adjutant-General, dated Horse Guards, 31st August, 1830.

1806 On the return of the regiment from India it was ordered to resume the kilt as its dress, and to proceed immediately to Scotland to recruit to the establishment, which was fixed as as follows:—

1 Colonel.	12 Lieutenants.
1 Lieutenant-Colonel.	8 Ensigns.
2 Majors.	1 Pay-Master.
10 Captains.	1 Adjutant.

1	Quarter-Master
1	Surgeon.
2	Assistant Surgeons.
1	Serjeant-Major.
1	Quarter-Master-Serjeant.
1	Pay-Master-Serjeant.
1	Armourer-Serjeant.
40	Serjeants.
40	Corporals.
20	Drummers.
2	Fifers.
760	Privates.
906	Total of all ranks, officers and men.

The regiment embarked for Scotland at Greenwich on the 2nd March, 1806, and was stationed at Dumbarton Castle, and afterwards at Glasgow, until the
1808 end of April, 1808, when it was ordered to Fort George, and arrived there in the end of May; there were at this time still 400 men wanting to complete it to its establishment. Although every exertion was made, and a number of recruiting parties stationed throughout the north of Scotland, they did not succeed well enough to fill up the ranks, by exclusively national recruiting, with sufficient rapidity, the call for regiments to proceed on active service being urgent. The regiment was then ordered to Ireland, and to be completed by volunteers from the English and Irish as well as Scotch regiments of militia. It marched from Fort George
1809 on the 29th January, 1809; embarked at Port Patrick

on the 1st March, and landing at Drogheda on the following day, proceeded to Newry. 1809

In the beginning of May, 1809, a notification was received from the Adjutant-General that the Highland dress of the regiment was to be discontinued in the following year, and that it was afterwards to be clothed and appointed as English regiments of the line; it however retained the designation of a Highland regiment until the year 1816.

Lieut.-Colonel Malcolm McPherson had succeeded Lieut.-Colonel Swinton in command of the regiment on its return from India; and on the 21st September, 1809, Lieut.-Colonel the Honourable Robert Le Poer Trench was appointed Lieut.-Colonel, from Inspecting Field Officer in Canada, by exchange with Lieut.-Colonel McPherson.

On the 19th December the regiment received a route for Fermoy, in order to embark for the Peninsula; it commenced its march from Newry in five divisions on the 21st December, 1809, and arrived at Fermoy on
the 11th January, 1810; marched for Cork on the 18th, 1810
embarked in four transports for the Peninsula, at Monkstown, on the 19th, and sailed from Cove on the 24th January.*

The transports entered the Tagus on the 5th February, the regiment was disembarked on the 10th, and stationed in the convent of San Benito, making arrangements for the campaign.

Major-General Picton, who about this time landed at Lisbon on his way to the army, inspected the regiment on the 20th February, and expressed himself much pleased with its appearance. On the 27th, the regiment

* For state of the regiment on embarkation, see Appendix No. 4, page 130.

1810 commenced its march from Lisbon to join the allied army under Lord Wellington, of which the head quarters were then at Viseu, proceeding by Santarem, Villa Franca, Alcoentra, Rio Mayor and Carvalhos to Leiria, where it was halted, on account of excessively heavy rains, from the 4th until the 10th of March, and thence marching by Pombal, Condeixa, Coimbra, Mealhada, Martigao and Tondella, reached Viseu on the 16th of March.

While halted at Viseu, Colonel Trench took an opportunity of communicating to the regiment a compliment paid to its character by the same illustrious Commander under whom it had served in the East, who had on the previous day inquired the number of men remaining with the corps who had fought at Assaye; and had told the Colonel, that "if the SEVENTY-FOURTH "would behave in that country as they had done in India, "he ought to be proud to command such a regiment."

The regiment having been detailed to the third (Major-General Picton's) division, which was then stationed at Pinhel, marched from Viseu on the 20th, and reached Pinhel on the 31st of March.

The 3rd Division was thus composed:—

1st Brigade, called Major-General Picton's, but commanded by Colonel Henry McKinnon, consisted of the first battalion 45th, the SEVENTY-FOURTH, the 88th, and three companies fifth battalion 60th regiments.

2nd Brigade, Major-General Lightburne's, 5th, second battalion 58th, and second battalion 83rd regiments.

The SEVENTY-FOURTH remained until the end of the war in the same division, bearing a distinguished part in all the services, which earned its well known

appellation of the Fighting Division. These services, 1810
and the great military operations for the emancipation of the Peninsula, in the course of which they were performed, are recorded in the general history of the war; and can never be forgotten until the fame of Wellington and the glories of the British arms shall have alike passed into oblivion. In the annals of any one regiment, however distinguished, these great operations can be noticed only to such an extent as may be indispensably necessary to indicate the precise occasions which called for its services.

At the commencement of 1810, the French, although driven from Portugal by the British victories of the previous year, had been largely reinforced, and had overrun and reduced to subjection nearly the whole of Spain, with a force of not less than 370,000 men and 80,000 horses. A part of this immense host, called the Army of Portugal, consisting of their 2nd, 6th and 8th corps, and numbering 87,000 men, was about to advance under one of Napoleon's most skilful Generals (Marshal Massena) with the confident and proud boast that they would drive the English into the sea. Lord Wellington had to oppose them only about 23,000 British troops, organised in five divisions of infantry and one of cavalry, but he had been appointed Marshal General of the Portuguese armies, which had been disciplined under British officers, and were in a fit state to give efficient aid in the defence of their country.

The allied forces were cantoned along the north-eastern frontier of Portugal, the light division being in advance between the rivers Coa and Agueda, watching the French movements, and the 3rd division in support of it at Pinhel.

The enemy commenced active operations by laying

1810 siege to the fortress of Ciudad Rodrigo in the beginning of June, but nothing to affect the 3rd division occurred during the siege, except that on the 19th of June the 1st brigade was sent to the banks of the Coa, and bivouacked there for ten days. The fortress surrendered on the 11th of July, and after the gallant but hazardous combat between the light division and the French advance on the 24th of July, they passed the Coa in overwhelming numbers, and the retrograde movement, and concentration of the allies behind the Mondego river, immediately commenced.

The SEVENTY-FOURTH, with the rest of the 3rd division, was drawn back to Linhares on the night of the 25th of July, and remained there until the 19th of August, on which day, the French being occupied with the siege of Almeida, it was advanced to Villa Franca; but Almeida having surrendered on the 27th, the allies were again withdrawn to their former positions. The French line of invasion was not finally indicated until the middle of September, when they commenced their advance into Portugal along the right bank of the Mondego.

Lord Wellington, notwithstanding their vastly superior numbers, determined to give them battle in the position of *Busaco*, a lofty and rugged sierra or mountain ridge, extending about eight miles in a northerly direction from the Mondego and crossing their line of march. The 3rd division, on the 21st of September, passed over the Mondego to Pena Cova, moved on the 22nd to a bivouac near Contisa at the foot of the sierra, and ascended in the afternoon of the 25th to the station it was to occupy in the approaching battle. On the 26th all the divisions of the allied army were assembled in their respective positions; the 2nd

(Lord Hill's) division on the extreme right guarding 1810 the declivities towards the Mondego; next to it the 5th (General Leith's) division; then the 3rd division, having the 1st (General Spencer's) division on its left, occupying the highest part of the ridge; then the light (General Craufurd's) division at the convent of Busaco; and the 4th (General Cole's) division on the extreme left. In front, within cannon shot and in full view of the Allied position, was assembled Marshal Massena's army, 70,000 strong, occupying the opposite range of mountains; the day passed over peaceably, but during the evening and night small parties of skirmishers, passing up the dark ravines, attempted to establish themselves close to the British line, and kept all upon the alert.

The position of Busaco, although formidable from the steepness and rugged character of its face, was too extensive to be completely occupied by the 25,000 British, and the same number of Portuguese troops, which formed the allied army, and there was an interval of about two miles between the left of the fifth and the right of the third division, which occupied the lowest and most accessible part of the position. The right brigade was thus distributed: the SEVENTY-FOURTH across the road leading from St. Antonio de Cantara to Coimbra, having two Portuguese guns on its right, and still further to the right the ninth and twenty-first Portuguese regiments. On the left of the SEVENTY-FOURTH was the eighth Portuguese, and beyond them the eighty-eighth and forty-fifth regiments, occupying the crest of a hill considerably to the left.

Shortly before daybreak on the 27th of September, the French formed five columns of attack, three of their 6th corps, under Marshal Ney, against the left of the British position, occupied by the light division, and two

1810 of their 2nd corps, under General Regnier, against the third division.

The advance of these two last-mentioned columns was preceded by a cannonade from fourteen pieces of artillery, which caused some casualties in the ranks of the regiment. Captain Langlands, of the SEVENTY-FOURTH, had a narrow escape; he was knocked down by a nine-pounder shot, which passed through his cap, and was supposed to be killed, but he rose again uninjured, and was congratulated by Major-General Picton on his good fortune. It being very trying to the young soldiers, of whom the SEVENTY-FOURTH regiment was chiefly composed, to be kept standing inactive when now under fire for the first time, Colonel Trench shortly addressed them, calling upon them to remember Assaye, and to imitate the former distinguished conduct of the regiment in India.

Both columns of the enemy advanced to the attack of the Allied position, with the usual impetuous rush of French troops, and preceded by a cloud of skirmishers. Of these columns the one to the left was, on reaching the top of the ridge, occupied by the eighty-eighth and forty-fifth regiments, attacked and driven back by them after a severe and gallant contest. Meanwhile, the other column advanced upon the SEVENTY-FOURTH, by the road from St. Antonio de Cantara; the two right companies of the regiment were immediately detached, with the Rifle companies belonging to the brigade, and drove back the enemy's skirmishers with great vigour, nearly to the foot of the Sierra.*

---

* Lieut. Alves, who belonged to one of those companies, says in his journal, "The pleasure I experienced in advancing after the "enemy, instead of remaining exposed and inactive as we were, can-"not be expressed." This officer (now Major of the Depôt Battalion in the Isle of Wight) was present with the SEVENTY-FOURTH during every march and service in which it was engaged, from its first landing

The first advance of the French column was repulsed 1810 by the close and steady fire of the regiment, aided by the ninth and twenty-first Portuguese, before it reached the top of the ridge; but the attack was renewed with greater numbers to force the road guarded by the SEVENTY-FOURTH; and the eighth Portuguese on its left, being thrown into confusion, the SEVENTY-FOURTH regiment was placed in a most critical situation, with its left flank exposed to the overwhelming force of the enemy. Fortunately, General Leith had observed the danger, and detached two regiments (the 9th and 38th) of the fifth division, which passing from the right, along the rear of the SEVENTY-FOURTH, in double quick time, the leading regiment (the 9th) met the head of the French column, just as it crowned the ridge, in the space vacated by the Portuguese, and drove them with irresistible force from the crest of the position down the precipice. The SEVENTY-FOURTH then advanced with the ninth, and kept up a fire upon the enemy as long as they could be reached. This attack, upon which the enemy had chiefly relied, having been thus repulsed, as well as those made by them upon the left of the allied position, the fate of the day was finally decided, and they desisted from further efforts, after sustaining a loss of above 5000 men killed and wounded.*

Major-General Picton, commanding the division,

in the Peninsula until its return home in 1814, without one single day's absence from the regiment throughout the period. To the journal kept by him, in which the date of every event was noted at the time it occurred, the accuracy of the Regimental Record is chiefly attributable. Major Alves has received the War Medal, and Clasps, for eleven battles.

* As different accounts have been frequently given regarding this part of the battle, a statement by Lieut. White (late Town-major of Portsmouth), who was present in the battle as Adjutant, and was stationed on the left and in rear of the regiment, of the occurrences which he personally observed, is given in the Appendix, No. 7, p. 140.

1810 gave the following account of the first attack upon the position defended by the SEVENTY-FOURTH, in a letter written immediately after the battle:—

"A sharp fire of musketry was heard on the left a "short time before daylight, and immediately after- "wards, fourteen pieces of cannon from an opposite "height opened upon the pass, and a large column "attempted to force it in mass; but so constant and "destructive a fire was kept up by the light corps of "the division on their flank, and by the SEVENTY- "FOURTH and a Portuguese battalion on their front, that "although they long persisted with great gallantry and "perseverance, they never were able to gain an inch of "ground, and were ultimately obliged to abandon the "attempt in great confusion.

"Convinced that the enemy would make no impres- "sion upon the pass of St. Antonio, from which they "were completely repulsed, I galloped towards the "left, &c., &c., &c."

The SEVENTY-FOURTH regiment, although so hotly and decisively engaged at the most important point of the position, did not sustain any great loss, the enemy having been chiefly repulsed by its fire before they could come to close quarters.

The casualties in the regiment were:—One officer, Ensign Williams, and seven rank and file, killed. One officer, Lieut. Cargill, and eighteen rank and file, wounded.* The SEVENTY-FOURTH regiment has received the Royal authority to bear the word "BUSACO" on the Regimental colour and appointments, in commemoration of its services in the battle.

On the following day there was some skirmishing at

* For non-commissioned officers and men killed and wounded, *see* Appendix, No. 6, page 134.

different points of the line, but the French, taught by 1810
experience to appreciate the strength of the position and the valour of its defenders, did not renew the assault. Towards evening their columns were seen in movement to their right, and their whole army was shortly on the march to turn the British left flank.

The allies then commenced their retreat, and before daybreak on the 29th, the position of Busaco was evacuated, the divisions moving on their previously arranged lines of retreat towards the lines of Torres Vedras.

The SEVENTY-FOURTH regiment marched on the 29th of September to Coimbra, on the 30th crossed the Mondego to Condeixa, and on the following days continued its march by Pombal, Leiria, Alcobaça, Caldas, and Obidos, and the pass of Roleia, to Torres Vedras, where it arrived on the 8th of October, and was cantoned within the stupendous line of entrenchments and fortifications, which had, by Lord Wellington's orders, been constructed, with admirable skill and immense labour, for the defence of Lisbon. The French general, who had followed the retreat through a wasted and deserted country, with the confident expectation that he was driving the British to their ships, found his progress arrested on the 10th of October by this barrier, which he soon perceived to be impregnable, and which extended twenty-nine miles from the Tagus to the sea. The regiment remained cantoned at Torres Vedras until the middle of December. Within the lines, supplies were abundant, and with the exception of some employment in strengthening the defensive works, amusements, exercises and field-sports of every attainable kind were the occupation of all ranks, who engaged in them as if no hostile interruption was to be apprehended.

The allied army was at this time augmented by

1810 additional regiments from England, and a sixth division of infantry added to it.*

Meanwhile the French had remained bivouacked in front of the lines, although exposed to terrible privations and hardships, until the 14th of November, when they withdrew to a formidable position at Santarem; a movement in advance from the lines was consequently made by the greater part of the allied army. The third division remained, however, stationary until the 18th of December, when the SEVENTY-FOURTH marched from Torres Vedras to Aldea Gallego, and thence on the following day to the village of Togarro, where the regiment was cantoned until the beginning of March,
1811 1811. During this period much discomfort and hardship was endured from the continued heavy rains, the scanty supply of provisions, miserably bad cantonments, and the want of any occupation or amusement, except the game of foot-ball, for either officers or men.

The French having determined to withdraw from Portugal, broke up from their position at Santarem on the night of the 5th of March, and retreated towards the Mondego. On the 6th, the allies followed in pursuit, and came up with them at Pombal on the 11th, but after some skirmishing, they retired from their position during the night. On the 12th of March, the pursuit was continued, and after an advance of about eight miles, a rear guard, consisting of a division under Marshal Ney, was found posted in front of the village of *Redinha*, its flanks being protected by wooded heights. The light division was sent to attack the heights on the right of the enemy, and the third division those on his left, which they did in skirmishing

* For establishment of the regiment, 25th of October, 1810, *see* Appendix, No. 5, page 132.

order, while the remainder of the allied army, thirty 1811
thousand strong, moved in two majestic lines across the plain. After a sharp skirmish, in which the SEVENTY-FOURTH had one private killed, and one officer, Lieut. Crabbe, and six rank and file wounded,* the enemy retired across the Redinha river. On the 13th of March at Condeixa, and on the 14th at Casal Novo, the third division was employed on the right of the allied advance, turning the left of the French positions. The enemy having retreated across the Ceira river, leaving a rear guard of twelve battalions, under Marshal Ney, posted at *Foz d'Aronce,* this body was attacked on the afternoon of the 15th of March, by the third and light divisions, and their left and centre were dispersed with great loss, and driven over the Ceira by a charge of the third division.

Captain Thomson and eleven rank and file of the SEVENTY-FOURTH were wounded in this affair.

Great privations were endured by the whole of the third division, which was constantly in advance on the right of the army during these operations; the supplies of provisions intended for them having been appropriated by some of the troops in the rear. This want of provisions caused a day's halt of the whole army on the Ceira. The French continued to retreat up the left of the Mondego, and the third division to move along the mountains parallel with that river, and pressing upon their flank, but the SEVENTY-FOURTH had no opportunity of performing any particularly distinguished service during these movements.

At Sabugal on the Coa, on the 3rd of April, the third, fifth, and light divisions attacked the second corps of

* For men killed and wounded at Redinha, *see* Appendix, No. 6, page 134.

1811 the French, posted there under General Regnier, and drove them from their position with great loss; the light division had, however, the chief share in this exploit. The French retreated from Ciudad Rodrigo, and on the 5th crossed the frontier of Portugal, having lost almost thirty thousand men during their unsuccessful invasion. The SEVENTY-FOURTH regiment was now advanced to Nave d'Aver, where it remained cantoned during the investment of Almeida by the allied army. Marshal Massena, having obtained reinforcements from the other French corps, advanced from Ciudad Rodrigo on the 2nd of May for the relief of Almeida. On this day, the SEVENTY-FOURTH advanced from Nave d'Aver, and bivouacked in rear of the village of *Fuentes d'Onor*, on the right of the position occupied by the allied army, which extended for about five miles along the Dos Casas river, and in which Lord Wellington determined to receive the attack of the enemy, although they outnumbered his force by more than one-third. The village of Fuentes is situated on low ground, at the bottom of a ravine, with an old chapel and some buildings on a craggy eminence at its nearer end. On the morning of the 3rd of May, the first and third divisions were concentrated on a gentle rise, a cannon shot in its rear.

The village was occupied by the light companies and detachments of the first, third, and fifth divisions, and by the second battalion eighty-third regiment; these, when hard pressed by the enemy, were reinforced by the twenty-fourth, seventy-first, and seventy-ninth regiments, which succeeded in driving back the French after a combat which lasted till night. The following day passed in manœuvres and occasional skirmishing, but on the 5th of May, shortly after daybreak, while various movements and changes of position were going on, and a sharp contest maintained in other parts of the field, the French renewed their attack with increased force upon the village of Fuentes, which continued to be occupied by the twenty-fourth, seventy-first, and seventy-ninth regiments, together with the light companies of the third division, and the piquets under Lieut.-Colonel Trench, of the SEVENTY-FOURTH. After a hard fight for the possession of the village, which lasted, with many changes of fortune, until about ten o'clock, the defenders, hardly pressed, were nearly driven out of it by the vastly superior numbers of the enemy, and the SEVENTY-FOURTH, under Major Manners, were ordered up to their assistance. 1811

The left wing alone was at first ordered to advance in double quick time. On approaching the village, it was directed to take ground to its right, and in doing so, after passing by the left of the seventy-ninth regiment, it narrowly escaped being cut off by a heavy column of the enemy, which was concealed in a lane, and was observed only in time to check the advance and to allow the wing to take cover behind some walls, where it maintained itself until about noon; when the right wing joined the left, and with the forty-fifth, seventy-first, seventy-ninth, and eighty-eighth regiments, under the command of Colonel McKinnon, charged through and drove the enemy from the village, which they never afterwards recovered, although the whole of their sixth corps was engaged in the attempt; firing was, however, kept up until sunset. No sooner had the bugles sounded to cease firing, than the men on both sides, exhausted by their exertions during this protracted struggle and by the heat of the day, crowded amicably for water to the Dos Casas river, and the enemy were allowed to carry off their wounded. The troops in the

1811 village being then relieved by the light division, the regiment was withdrawn to its former position.

The casualties in the SEVENTY-FOURTH on this day were :—killed, one officer, Ensign Johnston, one serjeant, and four rank and file; wounded, three officers, Captains Shawe, McQueen, and Adjutant White, and sixty-four rank and file.*

The SEVENTY-FOURTH regiment has received the Royal authority to bear on the Regimental colour and appointments the words "FUENTES D' ONOR," in commemoration of its services in this battle.

On the three following days the regiment remained stationary, and large working parties were employed in throwing up entrenchments to protect the right of the position behind the village of Fuentes, but the French did not renew the attack, and having failed in their attempt to relieve Almeida, re-crossed the Agueda on the 10th of May. Marshal Marmont then superseded Massena in his command of the army of Portugal.

The regiment was moved back to its former cantonments at Nave d' Aver, but marched from thence with the rest of the third and the seventh divisions on the 14th for *Badajoz*, and crossing the Tagus by boats to Niza on the 20th, reached Campo Mayor on the 23rd of May. It advanced from thence and crossed the Guadiana, above Badajoz, on the 28th. The second British siege of that fortress then commenced, with the attack of the castle by the third, and of San Christoval by the seventh division on the 30th May. The batteries opened on the 3rd June. The assaults of San Christoval by the seventh division on the 6th and 9th having failed, the siege was abandoned, and turned into a blockade

* For non-commissioned officers and men killed and wounded, *see* Appendix, No. 6, page 134.

on the 13th June; but the French army of Portugal, 1811
under Marshal Marmont, having now effected a junction with that of the south, under Marshal Soult, they advanced together to relieve Badajoz, and the Allied troops were withdrawn to Campo Mayor. On the 17th, the other divisions of the allies having arrived from the north, the whole army was placed upon the Caya river, and a great battle was expected; but the enemy having withdrawn, Marshal Soult to the south, and Marshal Marmont to the valley of the Tagus, the Allies commenced their return northward in the middle of July.

The SEVENTY-FOURTH regiment marched on the 18th July, reached *Albergaria* on the 9th August, and was there cantoned until the middle of September; during this period the allied army blockaded Ciudad Rodrigo. The regiment was, on the 17th September, advanced to El Bodon on the Agueda, and on the 22nd to Pastores, within three miles of Ciudad Rodrigo, forming, with the three companies of the 60th, the advanced guard of the third division, which occupied the central position of the allied army, the light division being on its right beyond the Agueda.

On the 23rd the French, under Marshal Marmont, advanced to Ciudad Rodrigo on the north-east side, and on the following day introduced a convoy.

On the 25th they advanced thirty squadrons of cavalry, fourteen battalions of infantry, and twelve guns, under General Montbrun, from Ciudad Rodrigo, direct upon the main body of the third division at El Bodon, and caused it to retire, surrounded and continually threatened by overwhelming numbers of cavalry, over a plain for six miles, to Guinaldo.

The SEVENTY-FOURTH, and the companies of the sixtieth, under Lieut.-Colonel Trench, at Pastores, were

1811 completely cut off from the rest of the division by the French advance, and were left without orders; but they succeeded in passing the Agueda by a ford, and making a very long detour through Robledo, where they captured a party of French cavalry, recrossed the Agueda, and joined the division in bivouac near Guinaldo, at about two o'clock on the morning of the 26th. It was believed at head-quarters that this detachment had been all captured, although Major-General Picton, much pleased at their safe return, said he thought he must have heard more firing before the SEVENTY-FOURTH could be taken. After a rest of an hour or two, the regiment was again under arms, and drawn up in position at Guinaldo before daybreak, with the remainder of the third and the fourth division. The French army, 60,000 strong, being united in their front, they retired at night about twelve miles to Alfayates. The regiment was again under arms at Alfayates throughout the 27th, during the skirmish in which the fourth division was engaged at Aldea de Ponte. On this occasion the men were so much exhausted by the continued exertions of the two preceding days, that one hundred and twenty-five of them were unable to remain in the ranks, and were ordered to a village across the Coa, where eighty died of fatigue. This disaster reduced the effective strength of the regiment below that of twelve hundred, required to form a second battalion, which had been ordered during the previous month, and the requisite strength was not again reached during the war.

During the night the allies moved to a position near Sabugal, on the Coa, but the enemy did not attack, and retired on the 28th.

The SEVENTY-FOURTH regiment was, with a few intervals, cantoned from the beginning of October at Aldea

de Ponte, where the whole of Major-General McKin- 1811
non's brigade was, after the beginning of December, employed in making fascines and gabions for the projected siege of *Ciudad Rodrigo.* Every preparation for the siege having been made with the utmost possible secrecy, the third division marched on the 4th January,
1812, and crossing the Agueda by the bridge of Villor, 1812
reached Robledo the same night. This was an exceedingly long and severe march, lasting from six o'clock in the morning until eleven at night, and the intense cold, heavy rain, and dreadfully bad roads, caused many men of all the regiments to be left behind, some of whom perished; but the SEVENTY-FOURTH, animated by the prospect of immediate service, were able to muster every man present on the following day.

On the 7th, the third division was cantoned in the village of Zamorra, about five miles from Ciudad Rodrigo, where it remained during the siege. There being no camp equipage or cover of any kind for the troops nearer than the villages in which they were cantoned, at distances varying from five to eight miles from Rodrigo, one of the divisions employed (the first, third, fourth, and light) marched from its cantonments, carrying cooked provisions, and relieved the preceding division at noon each day, remaining on the ground and furnishing all the guards of the trenches and working parties for twenty-four hours. The distances the men had to march, together with the extreme cold of the weather, which prevented their taking any rest during their tour of twenty-four hours' duty, rendered the work of the siege most laborious and trying. On the 8th January, in the evening, the light division stormed the redoubt *Renaud* on the hill called the *Upper Teson,* and opened the trenches. The third division had the duty of the

1812 trenches on the 11th and 15th, and again on the 19th of January, when two breaches having been reported practicable, although the counterscarp was still entire, the assault was ordered to take place at seven o'clock in the evening, by the third and light divisions. The assault of the great breach was confided to Major-General McKinnon's brigade, preceded by a storming party of five hundred men under Major Manners, of the SEVENTY-FOURTH, with a forlorn hope under Lieut. Mackie, of the eighty-eighth regiment. There were two columns of the fifth and ninety-fourth regiments ordered to attack and clear the ditch and *fausse-braie* on the right of the breach, the light division to storm the small breach on the left, and a false attack on the opposite side of the town to be made by Major-General Pack's Portuguese brigade.

Immediately after dark, Major-General Picton formed the third division in the first parallel and approaches, and lined the parapet of the second parallel with the eighty-third regiment, to cover the attack by its fire. At the appointed hour the attack commenced, and immediately a heavy discharge of musketry was opened from the trenches, under cover of which one hundred and fifty sappers, directed by two engineer officers, and Captain Thomson* of the SEVENTY-FOURTH, advanced from the second parallel to the crest of the glacis, carrying bags filled with hay, which they threw down the counterscarp into the ditch, and thus reduced its height from thirteen and a-half to eight feet; they then fixed the ladders, and the brigade, in conjunction with the fifth and ninety-fourth regiments, which arrived at the same moment along the ditch from the right, immediately

* Now Major-General Alexander Thomson, C.B.

SEVENTY FOURTH

REGIMENT.

Madeley lith. 3 Wellington St Strand

FOR CANNON'S MILITARY RECORDS.

pushed up the breach, and after a short struggle with the bayonet gained the summit; but the enemy had strongly retrenched it, and maintained a hot fire of musketry upon them from traverses on either side; the top of the breach was also raked with grape, from two guns flanking it at the distance of a few yards. The contest was short but severe; officers and men fell in heaps, killed and wounded, and many were thrown down the scarp into the main ditch, a depth of thirty feet; but by desperate efforts directed along the parapet on both flanks, the assailants succeeded in turning the retrenchments. The garrison then abandoned the rampart, having first exploded a mine in the ditch of the retrenchment, by which Major-General McKinnon and many of the bravest and most forward perished in the moment of victory. General Vandeleur's brigade of the light division had advanced at the same time to the attack of the lesser breach on the left, which, being without interior defence, was less obstinately disputed, and the fortress was won. 1812

Lord Wellington, in his despatch, dated 20th January, thus speaks of the third division:—

"The conduct of all parts of the third division, in "the operations which they performed with so much "gallantry and exactness on the evening of the 19th, "in the dark, affords the strongest proof of the abi- "lities of Lieut.-General Picton and Major-General "McKinnon, by whom they were directed and led; but "I beg particularly to draw your Lordship's attention to "the conduct of Lieut.-Colonel O'Toole, second Caça- "dores, Major Ridge, fifth foot, Lieut.-Colonel Camp- "bell, ninety-fourth, Major Manners, SEVENTY-FOURTH, "and of Major Grey, fifth foot, who has been twice "wounded during this siege.

1812 "It is but justice also to the third division to report, "that the men who performed the sap belonged to the "forty-fifth, SEVENTY-FOURTH, and eighty-eighth regi- "ments, under the command of Captain McLeod of "the Royal Engineers, and Captain Thomson of the "SEVENTY-FOURTH, Lieut. Beresford of the eighty- "eighth, and Lieut. Metcalfe of the forty-fifth; and "they distinguished themselves not less in the storm of "the place than they had in the performance of their "laborious duty during the siege."

The casualties in the regiment during the siege of Ciudad Rodrigo were:—killed, six rank and file; wounded, five officers, Captains Langlands and Collins, Lieutenants Tew and Ramadge, and Ensign Atkinson, two serjeants, and twenty-four rank and file.*

The SEVENTY-FOURTH have received the Royal authority to bear on the Regimental colour and appointments, the words "CIUDAD RODRIGO," in commemoration of their services at the capture of that fortress.

Major Manners received the brevet of Lieut.-Colonel for his services on this occasion.

The unlooked for rapidity with which this formidable fortress had been captured, astonished the French General, who had assembled an army of sixty thousand men for its relief, which now again retired to its winter quarters. On the day after the capture, the SEVENTY-FOURTH regiment returned to its cantonments at Zamorra, and in the beginning of February was moved to Legiosa. Meanwhile the defences of Ciudad Rodrigo were restored, and preparations secretly made for the siege of *Badajoz,* on which Lord Wellington had now determined. The army was put in movement for that des-

* For names of non-commissioned officers and men killed and wounded at Ciudad Rodrigo, *see* Appendix No. 6, page 135.

tination at the end of February. The SEVENTY-FOURTH 1812
marched on the 25th February, reached Elvas on the 15th March, and on the 16th crossed the Guadiana, two miles below Badajoz, when the enemy's piquets were driven in, and the place invested on the left of the Guadiana, by the third, fourth, and light divisions, and a brigade of Portuguese. On the 17th March the third division was stationed on the south-east side of the town, nearly on the ground it occupied at the former siege; and the men of the forty-fifth, SEVENTY-FOURTH, and eighty-eighth regiments, who had been employed as sappers at Ciudad Rodrigo, were again so employed at Badajoz.

The first parallel was on this night commenced opposite to Fort Picurina, and continued on the 18th, but the work was much impeded by continued heavy rain. On the 19th the garrison made a sortie with fifteen hundred infantry and a party of cavalry, from behind the Picurina, driving back the working party and guard of the trenches from the parallel; their cavalry penetrated to the engineer depôts, causing great confusion and some loss. The SEVENTY-FOURTH was the first regiment under arms, and advanced under Major-General Kempt (who had succeeded Major-General McKinnon in command of the brigade) in double quick time, to the plain on the right, opposite to the castle, and with the guard of the trenches, drove back the enemy, who sustained a loss of three hundred officers and men. The attack was continued as rapidly as possible, but was impeded by very heavy rain, which rendered the work in the trenches extremely laborious, until the 25th, when the batteries opened against the place. On this night Fort Picurina was assaulted and carried by five hundred men of the third

1812 division, two hundred of whom were under Major Shaw of the SEVENTY-FOURTH, two hundred under Major Rudd of the seventy-seventh, and one hundred under Captain Powis of the eighty-third regiment.

This strong and important outwork is in the form of a bastion of nearly two hundred feet faces and seventy feet flanks, the rear being closed by a front of fortification; there were seven pieces of ordnance mounted on the ramparts; and the garrison, of nearly three hundred men, was commanded by a colonel on the staff. The detachments advanced to the attack at ten o'clock, and immediately alarms were sounded in the town, rockets thrown up, and a fire opened from all the ramparts on the work. The obstacles to an escalade were great, and the resistance of the garrison most determined; but after a hot and doubtful contest, in which the assailants lost four officers and fifty men killed, and fifteen officers and two hundred and fifty men wounded, the work was carried. Of the garrison a few escaped, three officers and eighty men were made prisoners, but the greater part were killed in the fight.

Of the SEVENTY-FOURTH Captain Collins and Lieutenant Ramadge (acting engineer) were killed, and Major Shawe dangerously wounded; he, however, recovered, and received the brevet of Lieut.-Colonel for his share in this gallant exploit.

Immediately after the Picurina was taken, three battalions were moved up for its protection, a lodgment was made in it, and the second parallel was commenced, but not completed until the night of the 26th. The operations in the trenches were pushed forward with the greatest vigour, still under heavy rain, and the men consequently working ankle deep in mud.

On the 30th and 31st breaching batteries opened

against the Santa Maria and La Trinidad bastions; and the breaches having been reported practicable on the 5th of April, the assault was ordered to take place at ten o'clock on the night of the 6th. "Then," in the words of Napier, "the soldiers eagerly made themselves "ready for a combat so furiously fought, so terribly "won, so dreadful in all its circumstances, that pos- "terity can scarcely be expected to credit the tale, but "many are still alive who know that it is true." 1812

It was ordered, that on the right, the third division was to file out of the trenches, to cross the Rivillas river, and to scale the castle walls, which were from eighteen to twenty-four feet high, furnished with all means of destruction, and so narrow at top that the defenders could easily reach and overturn the ladders.

On the left, the 5th division was to make a false attack on the Pardaleras outwork, and a real assault on the Bastion San Vincente.

In the centre, the fourth division was to assault the breach in the face of the Bastion La Trinidad, and the light division that in the flank of the Bastion Santa Maria.

The third division was drawn up on the extreme right, close to the Rivillas river, waiting the signal to attack, when a lighted carcass, thrown from the castle, discovered them to the enemy, and obliged them, and also the other assaulting columns, to anticipate the signal by about half an hour. They advanced on the night of the 6th April, at about half-past nine o'clock, led by Major-General Kempt,* across the Rivillas by a narrow bridge in single file, under a terrible fire from all the eastern works, and re-forming, ascended the hill to the foot of the castle wall with perfect regularity. Here General

* Now General the Right Honorable Sir James Kempt, G.C.B., Colonel of the First or Royal Regiment of Foot.

1812 Kempt fell wounded, and was carried to the rear, and General Picton, who had just come up, assumed the command of the division. The assailants now spreading along the front, endeavoured to plant their ladders, some against the castle walls and some against the adjoining front on the left; but the opposition to an escalade was most obstinate. The defenders, by means of logs of wood, large stones, and loaded shells, ranged along the parapet, crushed those employed to rear the foremost ladders, and shot and bayoneted all who ascended those that were first fixed. By the perseverance and determined exertions of Lieut.-General Picton and the officers of the division, fresh men were continually brought up as the foremost fell, and an entrance was at last forced by one ladder; this being effected, the resistance slackened, and the remaining ladders were quickly reared, by which the men ascended, and established themselves on the ramparts.

Lieutenant Alexander Grant of the SEVENTY-FOURTH, led the advance at the escalade, and on getting into the castle, went on with a few men through the gate into the town, but his small party was met and driven back by superior numbers; on his return he was unfortunately shot by a French soldier concealed in the gateway, and mortally wounded in the head; he was able, however, to descend the ladder, and was carried to the bivouac, and trepanned, but died two days afterwards. Another among the foremost in the escalade was John McLauchlan, the regimental piper, who, the instant he mounted the castle wall, began playing on his pipes the regimental quick step, "The Campbells are coming," at the head of the advance along the ramparts, as coolly as if on a common parade, until his music was stopped by a shot through the bag; he was afterwards seen by an officer of the regiment seated on a gun-

carriage quietly repairing the damage, regardless of 1812
the shot flying about him; and presently recommenced his animating tune.

Immediately after the escalade, according to the instructions previously received from Major-General Kempt, thirty or forty men of the SEVENTY-FOURTH were sent under Lieutenant Alves to the gate, with orders to close it, which they did with stones and rubbish; this was scarcely accomplished, when an unsuccessful attempt was made by a strong body from the town to force an entrance by the gate, now barricaded against them.

During the escalade of the castle, the heroic assaults on the retrenched breaches by the fourth and light divisions had been made and repulsed, when about midnight, after two thousand men had fallen, Lord Wellington, who was on a height close to the quarries, sent orders to the Commanding Officer to retire, and form for a fresh effort, a little before daybreak. Immediately after this order was issued Lieut.-General Picton's aide-de-camp arrived to report that the third division was in the castle, and received orders for Lieut.-General Picton to blow down the gates, but otherwise to remain quiet until morning, when he should sally out with two thousand men at the time of the assault.

The capture of the castle, however, and the escalade of the Bastion St. Viciente, by the fifth division, having turned the retrenchments, there was no further resistance, and the fourth and light divisions marched into the town by the breaches.

The third division remained under arms in the castle until daylight, when the gate was opened, and permission given to enter the town.

The storming of Badajoz, in which the SEVENTY-FOURTH took so distinguished a part, was probably the

1812 most celebrated of the many gallant exploits performed by the Peninsular army, and is thus spoken of by the highest authorities on the subject.

Sir John Jones, after describing the defences of the castle, says:—"In ordinary military reasoning, such a "spot would be considered secure from assault, but the "efforts of British troops occasionally set all calculation "at defiance; and when a few years shall have swept "away the eye-witnesses of their achievements on this "night, they will not be credited."*

And the historian of the Peninsular war thus ends his eloquent narrative of this siege, and of some distinquished traits of individual heroism:—

"Nor would I be understood to select these as pre-"eminent; many and signal were the other examples of "unbounded devotion, some known, some that will "never be known; for in such a tumult much passed "unobserved, and often the observers fell themselves, "ere they could bear testimony to what they saw; but "no age, no nation, ever sent forth braver troops to "battle than those who stormed Badajoz." †

Lord Wellington, in his despatch, thus particularly mentions the third division:—

"It is impossible that any expression of mine can con-"vey to your Lordship the sense which I entertain of the "gallantry of the officers and troops upon this occasion.

"The officers and troops of the third division have "distinguished themselves as usual in these operations. "Lieut.-General Picton has reported to me particularly "the conduct of Lieut.-Colonel the Hon. R. Le Poer "Trench and Lieut.-Colonel Manners of the SEVENTY-"FOURTH."

* Journal of Sieges in Spain.

† Napier's History of the Peninsular War.

The following Division Order was issued by Lieut.-General Picton :— 1813

"*Camp before Badajoz*, 8*th April*, 1812.

"The escalade of the Castle of Badajoz is another "proof of the invincible spirit of the third division; "it was an enterprise of a most arduous nature, and "nothing less than the spirit of heroism which has on "all occasions actuated the officers and soldiers of the "several corps composing the division, could have "brought it to so glorious and happy a conclusion.

"The commanding officers of regiments are entitled "to great credit for their exertions during the arduous "struggle and for the excellent order and discipline "they preserved in their respective corps after the "capture of the place.

"The whole conduct of the officers of every rank, and "that of the non-commissioned officers and soldiers "engaged on the occasion, is calculated to increase the "Lieut. General's confidence and admiration.

"This brilliant achievement has not been effected "without the loss of valuable officers and brave soldiers, "but they have merited well of their country, and have "fallen crowned with glory, as much objects of envy as "subjects of regret to their comrades."

The casualties in the regiment during the siege were:—Killed, three officers, Captain Collins, Lieutenants Ramadge and Grant, 1 serjeant, and 22 rank and file. Wounded, ten officers, Lieut.-Colonel the Honorable R. Le Poer Trench, Captain Langlands, Brevet-Major Shawe, Captains Thomson and Wingate, Lieutenants Lyster, Pattison, King, and Ironside, Ensign Atkinson, 7 serjeants, and 91 rank and file.*

---

* For non-commissioned officers and men killed and wounded at Badajoz, *see* Appendix No. 6, page 135.

1812 Captains Langlands and Thomson, of the SEVENTY-FOURTH, received the brevet rank of Major for their services at the siege, and Brevet-Major Shawe that of Lieut.-Colonel, for the capture of the Picurina Fort as already mentioned. The regiment has received the Royal authority to bear on the regimental colour and appointments, the word "BADAJOZ," in commemoration of its services at this siege.

Lieut.-Colonel Trench having been wounded at the assault of Badajoz, the command of the regiment devolved on Lieut.-Colonel Manners. It remained in bivouac at Badajoz until the 11th of April, when it marched for the north, arrived at Pine-dona on the frontiers of Beira on the 7th of May, and was cantoned there until the beginning of June. Lord Wellington, having completed his preparations for assuming the offensive, advanced against Marshal Marmont, whose head-quarters were at Salamanca. The SEVENTY-FOURTH marched from their cantonments on the 5th of June, crossed the Agueda by the ford of Carpillo on the 10th, and the Tormes, by the ford of Los Cantos, on the 17th, on which day the forts of Salamanca were invested by the sixth division. The remainder of the army was formed in order of battle on the heights of San Christoval, in front of Salamanca, from the 20th to the 28th of June, to meet Marshal Marmont, who advanced with 40,000 men to relieve the forts, and several skirmishes and changes of position took place; the forts, however, were captured on the 27th. Brevet-Major Thomson of the SEVENTY-FOURTH was employed as engineer at the siege of these forts. At this time Lieut.-General Picton left the army on leave of absence, and the command of the third division was entrusted to Major-General the Honorable Edward Pakenham.

The allied army then advanced in pursuit of Marshal 1812
Marmont, who retired across the Douro. The third division was bivouacked at the ford of Pollos, on the Douro, from the 3rd of July, watching the French, who occupied the opposite bank of the river, but on the 16th, Marshal Marmont having received reinforcements, crossed the Douro, and the allies retired, skilfully manœuvring and taking up different positions in presence of the enemy until, on the 21st, they reached the ground they formerly occupied, on the height of San Christoval. In the evening the third division and some Portuguese cavalry bivouacked, and entrenched themselves near the village of Cabrerizos, on the right bank of the Tormes, while the rest of the army passed the river by the bridge of Salamanca and the fords, and was placed in position covering Salamanca, with the right upon one of the two rocky hills called the *Arapiles*, and the left upon the Tormes. On the 22nd of July, at daylight, the third division was also moved across the Tormes, and placed in advance of the extreme right of a second line which was taken up by the allied army, nearly at right angles with its first position, in consequence of the seizure by the French of the outer of the two Arapiles, whereby they had obtained the power of cutting off the line of retreat upon Ciudad Rodrigo. The change of the allied position and various manœuvres occupied the day without any close engagement, excepting on the left for the possession of the Arapiles, and the battle of *Salamanca* did not commence in earnest until after three o'clock, when the third division was ordered to advance in four columns, supported by cavalry, to turn the French left, which had been very much extended by the advance of the division of General Thomières, with the light cavalry and fifty pieces of artillery, along a range of heights parallel with the British

1812 line, to cut off the right of the Allies from the Ciudad Rodrigo road. The attack of the third division was made in a most brilliant style. The open columns advancing, formed lines in the march, and fell upon the French, who, expecting to see the British in retreat towards Ciudad Rodrigo, were confounded by the unlooked-for blow. Their artillery, however, poured showers of grape into the ranks of the allies, and their skirmishers kept up a constant fire, but the division continued its steady advance, and was upon them before they could form line, driving them in confusion from the field; the regiments then wheeled back into column, allowed the cavalry to pass through, and immediately resumed their advance. The advance in line of the SEVENTY FOURTH for upwards of three miles attracted particular notice, and was much applauded by Major-General Pakenham, who frequently exclaimed, "Beautifully done, SEVENTY-FOURTH; beautiful, SEVENTY-FOURTH!" *

Lord Londonderry says, in his Story of the Peninsular War:—

"The attack of the third division was not only the "most spirited, but the most perfect thing of the kind "that modern times have witnessed. Regardless "alike of a charge of cavalry and of the murderous "fire which the enemy's batteries opened, on went these "fearless warriors, horse and foot, without check or "pause, until they won the ridge, and then the infantry "giving their volley, and the cavalry falling on, sword "in hand, the French were pierced, broken, and discomfited. So close indeed was the struggle, that in "several instances the British colours were seen waving "over the heads of the enemy's battalions."

The evolutions of this great battle, in which the

* Major Alves's Journal.

third division and the SEVENTY-FOURTH regiment bore 1812
so conspicuous a part, were too varied to be clearly described with brevity; but while the combat still raged in the centre, the third division continued its victorious advance upon the enemy's left, greatly assisted by the splendid charges made by Major-General Le Marchant's Brigade of heavy cavalry, regarding which Major-General Sir Charles Dalbiac says, in his memoir upon the subject:—

"Throughout these charges upon the enemy, the "heavy brigade was unsupported by any other portion "of the cavalry, but was followed, as rapidly as it "was possible for infantry to follow, by the third "division, which had so gloriously led the attack in "the first instance, and had so effectively turned the "enemy's extreme left."

In less than half an hour after the attack of the third division, and before the French had even formed in order of battle, their Commander-in-Chief (Marmont) and two generals had fallen, and the left of their army was turned and thrown into confusion. Of the division of Thomières, originally 7000 strong, 2000 had been taken prisoners, with two eagles and eleven pieces of cannon, and but a small number of fugitives escaped. Their right, however, still continued to resist until it was dark, but they were finally driven from the field, and after sustaining great loss, retreated through the woods across the Tormes, pursued by the first and light divisions, which had been kept in reserve.

Napier concludes his account as follows:—

"The battle of Salamanca, remarkable in many "points of view, was not least so in this, that it was the "first decided victory gained by the allies in the Penin-"sula. In former actions the French had been re-"pulsed, here they were driven headlong, as it were,

1812 " before a mighty wind, without help or stay, and the " results were proportionate."

The casualties in the regiment at the battle of Salamanca were :—Killed, three rank and file. Wounded, two officers, Brevet-Major Thomson and Lieutenant Ewing, both severely ; two serjeants, and forty-two rank and file.* The SEVENTY-FOURTH has received the Royal authority to bear on the regimental colour and appointments, the word " SALAMANCA," in commemoration of its services in this battle.

The French army, having, after its defeat, escaped over the Tormes on the night of the 22nd of July, under the Command of General Clausel, was followed by the allies over the Douro. While the left wing continued the pursuit of the French, the right wing of the allied army, to which the third division belonged, advanced under Lord Wellington on the 1st of August against the French army of the centre, which, under King Joseph, retreated upon Madrid. The allies entered that capital on the 13th of August, and were received with the utmost enthusiasm and joy by the inhabitants.

Although the French had evacuated Madrid, they had left a garrison of 2000 men, with a large quantity of stores, in the Fort La China, and entrenchments surrounding the Retiro, which was invested by the third and seventh divisions on the evening of the 13th of August. On the 14th, the regiment, with the rest of the third division, got under arms at four o'clock, A.M., to storm the fort, but the garrison capitulated.

Lieut.-Colonel Manners (Major) of the SEVENTY-FOURTH was appointed commandant.

The third and light divisions remained in garrison

* For non-commissioned officers and privates killed and wounded at Salamanca, *see* Appendix No. 6, page 136.

at Madrid until the 20th of October. The other divisions of the army were moved to the Escurial on the 18th of August, but were shortly afterwards (excepting the fourth division) sent to Arrevalo, and Lord Wellington himself left Madrid on the 1st of September to take the command. The advance to Burgos then took place, and the siege of the *Castle of Burgos* from the 19th of September until the 22nd of October, when the siege was raised, and the army commenced its retreat. 1812

The time passed most agreeably while the troops occupied Madrid, and the temporary change from the hardships of a campaign to the pleasures of a metropolis was delightful to all ranks. But although there were amusements and gaieties in abundance, the city exhibited a sad combination of luxury and desolation ; there was no money, the people were starving, and even noble families secretly sought charity.

Towards the end of September, when the distress was very great, the officers of the forty-fifth and SEVENTY-FOURTH regiments, feeling the utmost compassion for numbers of miserable objects who were worthy of a better fate, commenced giving a daily dinner to about two hundred of them, among whom were some persons of high distinction, who, without this resource, must have perished. Napier says, on this subject, that "the Madrilenos "discovered a deep and unaffected gratitude for kindness "received at the hands of the British officers, who contributed, not much, for they had it not, but enough of "money to form soup charities, by which hundreds were "succoured. Surely this is not the least of the many "honorable distinctions those brave men have earned."

About the middle of October, the French army, under Marshal Soult, having joined King Joseph, they advanced upon Madrid, and Lieut.-General Hill, with his

1812 corps of the allied army, being at Toledo, moved to his left, covering Madrid, and the troops in garrison there were advanced to join him.

The advanced guard of the French armies having passed the Tagus on the 29th of October, the retreat of the allies by the Guadarama was commenced. On the 30th the regiment marched past Madrid, without entering the city. The troops, retiring from Madrid, continued their march under General Hill, followed by the French, until the 8th of November, when they crossed the Tormes, and bivouacked on the field of the battle of Salamanca. The remainder of the army, retiring from Burgos under Lord Wellington, arrived on the same day, and on the 14th the whole were united in position on the two Arapiles, but on the 15th continued their retreat upon Ciudad Rodrigo, where they arrived on the 19th. The hardships and privations endured during these four days were very great, the marches being over almost impassable roads and marshy plains, under a continued deluge of rain, provisions deficient, and no shelter procurable. Many men died from exposure, and in the SEVENTY-FOURTH, of thirty-four men who had joined the regiment from England at Salamanca on the 14th, only four or five reached Ciudad Rodrigo. The retreat from Burgos and Madrid, and the campaign of 1812 having now ended, the army was placed in winter quarters behind the Agueda.

1813 The SEVENTY-FOURTH regiment was cantoned at Sarzedo, in the province of Beira, from the 6th December, 1812, until the 15th May, 1813. In the month of January, 1813, Major-General Colville, having rejoined his brigade, assumed the command of the third division. During the time passed in winter quarters, reinforcements of men and horses were received from England; a pontoon train was formed, tents were also supplied for the first time since the commencement of the war, in the proportion of three to each company; tin camp-kettles, carried by the men, one for every six men, were substituted for the heavy iron ones hitherto used, and the whole army was reorganised in greater strength than before, preparatory to the execution of Lord Wellington's grand plan for the expulsion of the French from the Peninsula. Before the commencement of the campaign, the men's great-coats were given into store, and blankets only ordered to be carried by them. 1813

In consequence of time lost in bringing up the pontoon train from Almeida, the advance into Spain, intended to commence on the 1st, was delayed until the middle of May.

The SEVENTY-FOURTH proceeded with the left column of the army, consisting of the first, third, fourth, fifth, sixth, and seventh divisions, with cavalry, artillery, and Portuguese troops, amounting to above 40,000 men, under Sir Thomas Graham. This column crossed the Douro, and marched by the right bank of that river; while the second and light divisions, with cavalry, artillery, and Portuguese and Spanish troops, amounting to about 25,000 men, and the head-quarters of the army, in two columns, advanced across the Tormes under Lord Wellington, and effected their junction with the left column by crossing the Douro at Toro. The whole army was united on the right bank of the river on the 3rd of June.

Lieut.-General Sir Thomas Picton had rejoined from England on the 20th May, and issued an order on assuming the command of the third division, from which the following is an extract:—

"D. O. " *Villa Flor, 20th May*, 1813.

"No. 1. Lieutenant General Sir Thomas Picton is

1813 "much gratified at finding himself again at the head "of a division which has signalized itself on so many "occasions, and which has never failed of complete "success in any one of the important enterprises it has "been employed upon.

"No. 2. From a continuance of the same spirit, good "humour and unanimity, the Lieut.-General con- "fidently anticipates equally brilliant results during "the operations of the present campaign."

The third division now consisted of three brigades, *viz.*, right brigade under Major-General Brisbane (as formerly), of the 1st battalion, 45th regiment, SEVENTY FOURTH, 88th, three companies 5th battalion 60th rifles; centre brigade, Lieut.-General Picton, 1st battalion 5th, 2nd battalion 83rd, 2nd battalion 87th, and 94th regiments; left brigade, Major-General Power, 9th, 11th, and 21st Portuguese regiments.

On the 4th of June the allies advanced, following the French armies of Portugal, and of the south and centre, which now, united under King Joseph, were in full retreat upon Burgos, where it was expected they would have made a stand; they, however, continued their retreat from Burgos over the Arlanzan river, after blowing up the castle and removing their stores, on the 12th of June. They then crossed the Ebro, and having assembled all the encumbrances, convoys, and stores of their armies at Vittoria, they entered that position on the 19th of June by the narrow mountain defile of Puebla, through which the river Zadora, after passing the city of Vittoria, and running through the valley in a winding course, flows towards the Ebro.

The Allied army, amounting to about 60,000 British and Portuguese of all arms, with about 20,000 Spanish auxiliaries, was, on the 20th of June, encamped on the banks of the river Bayas, behind the range of hills bounding the position of Vittoria, and about six miles 1813 distant from the Zadora.

The French, about 70,000 strong, with one hundred and fifty-two pieces of artillery, were now thus posted: their right in front of the city of Vittoria, where King Joseph's head-quarters were established; the centre, in front of the village of Arinez, was about six miles distant from, and nearly at right angles to their right, covered by the Zadora, and by an easy range of heights; while the right centre was upon a high hill near the village of Margarita, which commanded the whole valley. The extreme left of the French army was upon the Puebla mountain, facing the defile of that name. There was a large force in a second line, and the cavalry and the King's guards in reserve in rear of the centre, which was intended to defend the passage of the river Zadora, by the bridges of Mendoza, Tres Puentes, Villodas, and Nanclares; fifty pieces of artillery were also massed at the centre for the defence of these bridges.

On the 21st of June Lord Wellington ordered an attack to be made on three separate points: on the right by Lieut.-General Sir Rowland Hill, with the second division, upon the French left at Puebla; while on the left, Lieut.-General Sir Thomas Graham, with the first and fifth divisions, was to make a wide detour to the left, and crossing the Zadora at *Vittoria*, to attack their right, and cut off their retreat by the great road to Bayonne. The centre, consisting of the fourth and light divisions (under Lord Wellington himself) on the right, and the third and seventh, (under Lieut.-General the Earl of Dalhousie) on the left, was to pass the bridges in front, and attack as soon as the movements on the flanks should be executed. The troops moved from the camp on the Bayas at daybreak; the contest was at first chiefly

1813 on the extreme right and left, because, on account of the rugged nature of the ridges they had to pass, the left centre column, (third and seventh divisions,) did not reach the Zadora until nearly one o'clock, and the right centre, which had taken possession of the three lower bridges, was not able to advance far in the attack until the left should be ready to join it. The right brigade of the third division, followed by the seventh division, then crossed the bridge of Mendoza, the other brigades of the third division fording higher up the river.

The seventh division, and the centre brigade of the third division, then attacked the French right centre, in front of the villages of Margarita and Hermandad, and Lord Wellington, seeing the hill in front of the village of *Arinez*, weakly occupied by the enemy, ordered the right brigade of the third division, under Lieut.-General Picton, in close columns of battalions at a run diagonally across the front of both armies to that central point. The hill was carried immediately, and the French withdrew under cover of a cannonade from fifty pieces of artillery and a crowd of skirmishers, to the second range of heights, on which their reserve had been posted; they, however, still held the village of Arinez on the great road leading to Vittoria. The brigade then advanced to the attack of the village of *Arinez*; the three right companies of the SEVENTY-FOURTH, under Captain McQueen, with the companies of the sixtieth, immediately dashed forward and charged through the village, drove the enemy from it, and captured three guns; these companies were then halted under cover of some houses until the remainder of the regiment and brigade should come up, as the enemy were again advancing upon the post with increased numbers, and kept up a terrible fire of artillery

and musketry. The French were finally driven back in 1813
confusion at the point of the bayonet.

The SEVENTY-FOURTH received particular praise from both Lieut.-General Picton and Major-General Brisbane, commanding the division and brigade, for its alacrity in advancing and charging through the village of Arinez.

By the capture of the village, the great road was gained, and the troops on the French extreme left were turned, while they were hard pressed by Lieut.-General Sir Rowland Hill's attack on their front; the whole now retreated in confusion before the British advancing lines towards Vittoria, but as the ground was exceedingly diversified, being in some places wooded, in others open, and in others cut up by ditches, vineyards, and enclosures, they recovered their order, and the action for six miles became a running fight and cannonade. The regular and beautiful advance in line of the SEVENTY-FOURTH over this long distance was greatly admired, and was much attributable to the coolness and gallantry of the officer (Lieut. Davies), who carried the colours, and whenever the regiment got into broken ground, was the first on the bank, and stood with the colours until it was formed on his right and left. During this advance, the piper, McLauchlan, whose gallantry at the escalade of Badajoz has been before mentioned, was cut in two by a cannon shot, while playing in rear of the colours.* Many guns were taken as the army advanced. At six o'clock the French reached the last defensible height, one mile in front of Vittoria; here they made a stand, and the armies of the south and centre kept up a heavy fire, and above eighty pieces of cannon thundered upon the third division, which, being the foremost, bore the brunt of the fiery storm, until the fourth division carried a hill on

* Major Alves's Journal.

1813 the French left, when the enemy abandoned the position.

The Royal Causeway to Bayonne being blocked up by a confused mass of carriages, men, women, and children, the French retreated by the road to Salvatierra and Pampeluna, but this road being also blocked up, all became disorder, and they abandoned their artillery (except two pieces), equipages, stores, and papers: generals and subordinate officers being alike reduced to the clothes on their backs.*

The bâton of Marshal Jourdan, a stand of colours, one hundred and fifty-one pieces of brass ordnance, all the parks and depôts from Madrid, Valladolid, and Burgos, all their carriages, ammunition and treasure fell into the hands of the victors.†

The French regiments, which effected their escape from this total rout, arrived at Pampeluna, and took shelter in a defile beyond it in a state of complete disorganisation; darkness and the nature of the ground (unfavourable for cavalry) alone permitted their escape. At the distance of two leagues from Vittoria the pursuit was given up, and the allies halted for the night.

Sir Thomas Picton, in a letter of the 1st of July, thus speaks of his division:—

"On the 16th of May the division was put in move- "ment; on the 18th we crossed the Douro, on the 15th "of June the Ebro, and on the 21st fought the battle "of Vittoria. The third division had, as usual, a very "distinguished share in this decisive action. The "enemy's left rested on an elevated chain of craggy "mountains, and their right on a rapid river, with "commanding heights in the centre, and a succession "of undulating grounds, which afforded excellent situa-

* Napier. † Ibid.

" tions for artillery ; and several good positions in front 1813
" of Vittoria, where King Joseph had his head-quarters. " The battle began early in the morning, between our " right and the enemy's left on the high craggy heights, " and continued with various success for several hours. " About twelve o'clock the third division was ordered " to force the passage of the river and carry the heights " in the centre, which service was executed with so " much rapidity, that we got possession of the com- " manding ground before the enemy were aware of our " intention. The enemy attempted to dislodge us with " great superiority of force, and with forty or fifty " pieces of cannon. At that period the troops on our " right had not made sufficient progress to cover our " right flank, in consequence of which we suffered a " momentary check, and were driven out of a village " whence we had dislodged the enemy, but it was " quickly recovered; and on Sir Rowland Hill's (the " second) division, with a Portuguese and Spanish " division, forcing the enemy to abandon the heights, " and advancing to protect our flanks; we pushed the " enemy rapidly from all his positions, forced him to " abandon his cannon, and drove his cavalry and " infantry in confusion beyond the city of Vittoria " We took one hundred and fifty-two pieces of cannon, " the military chest, ammunition and baggage; besides " an immense treasure, the property of the French " generals, amassed in Spain.

" The third division was the most severely and per- " manently engaged of any part of the army; and we " in consequence sustained a loss of nearly eighteen " hundred killed and wounded, which is more than a " third of the total loss of the whole army."

The following Division and Brigade Orders were

1813 issued by Lieut.-General Sir Thomas Picton and Major-General Brisbane after the battle of Vittoria :—

"*23rd June*, 1813.

"DIVISION ORDERS.

"Lieut.-General Sir Thomas Picton congratulates "Major-General the Hon. Sir C. Colville, Major-"General Brisbane, and Major-General Power, upon "the conspicuous services rendered by the brigades "under their several commands, towards the brilliant "success of the 21st of June instant. He requests to "assure the commanding officer, officers, non-commis-"sioned officers and men of their corps and regiments, "that their conduct did not fail to excite his warm "admiration, and to increase the confidence he has "always felt in the command of the third division, &c."

"*Camp, Salvatierra*,
23rd June, 1813.

"BRIGADE ORDERS.

"Major-General Brisbane has reason to be highly "pleased with the conduct of the brigade in the action "of yesterday, but he is at a loss to express his admira-"tion of the conduct of the Honorable Colonel Le Poer "Trench and the SEVENTY-FOURTH regiment, which he "considers contributed much to the success of the day."

The casualties in the regiment at the battle of Vittoria were :—Killed, seven rank and file ; wounded, five officers, Captains McQueen and Ovens, Adjutant White, and Ensigns Hamilton and Shore, four serjeants, one drummer, and thirty-one rank and file.*

Captain William Moore received the brevet of Major for his conduct in this action.

The SEVENTY-FOURTH has received the Royal authority to bear on the regimental Colour and Appointments

* For non commissioned officers, drummers, and privates killed and wounded at Vittoria, *see* Appendix No. 6, page 137.

the word "VITTORIA" in commemoration of its services 1813
in the battle.

The allies followed in pursuit of the fugitive enemy to beyond Pampeluna, from the 22nd until the 25th, when they passed into the Pyrenees by the valley of Roncesvalles. Sir Thomas Graham was detached, with the first division, to the left, towards Guipuscoa, on the 23rd of June; and on the 26th, Lord Wellington, leaving the second division to blockade Pampeluna, marched with the third, fourth, seventh, and light divisions towards Tudela, to intercept General Clausel, who was on his way with a corps of 14,000 of the French army to join King Joseph at Vittoria; but General Clausel having made his escape by forced marches, the divisions returned to Pampeluna, and joined in the blockade on the 3rd July. The SEVENTY-FOURTH remained thus employed until the 16th. On the 15th July a reconnoitring party of the garrison was driven in by the piquets and SEVENTY-FOURTH, under Colonel Trench; the regiment sustained a loss on this occasion of three rank and file killed, and one serjeant and six rank and file wounded, from having followed the enemy too close to the walls of the fortress.

On the 17th of July the blockade of Pampeluna was entrusted to the Spaniards. The whole frontier of the Pyrenees, from the pass of Roncesvalles to the mouth of the Bidassoa river, was now occupied by the second, seventh, and light divisions, with some Portuguese brigades in the front line; and by the third, fourth and sixth divisions as supports, covering the blockade of *Pampeluna*, and the siege of *St. Sebastian* then going on under Lieut.-General Sir Thomas Graham. On the 18th the SEVENTY-FOURTH were encamped at Olague, in support of the central position, occupied by the second division at Bastan.

1813 Marshal Soult, having arrived at Bayonne on the 13th of July to command, as Lieutenant of the Emperor, the united French army of Spain, amounting to above 78,000 men, exclusive of garrisons, collected more than 60,000 men on his own left, and advanced on the 25th to force the pass of Roncesvalles. The fourth division, which was moved up in support of the front line of the allies, having been compelled to to retire after a day's hard fighting among the rocks and mountains, was joined on the 26th by the third division in advance of Zibiri; both divisions then continued to retire under the command of Lieut.-General Sir Thomas Picton, and on the morning of the 27th of July took up a position in front of Pampeluna, across the mouth of the Zibiri and Lanz valleys; the third division was posted on the right at Huarte, but was not severely engaged, the attacks of the enemy on the 28th being made chiefly upon the left of the position occupied by the fourth and sixth divisions, and the seventh and second divisions, which now arrived and were posted in position, still further to the left. During the night of the 29th the enemy drew to his right the troops immediately in front of the third division, in order to a formidable attack which he made on the 30th of July upon the second division, to turn the British left; Lord Wellington thereupon ordered an advance upon the enemy's position by the third, fourth and seventh divisions. Accordingly, at daylight on the 30th, the third division, with two squadrons of cavalry and a battery of artillery, advanced rapidly up the valley of Zibiri, skirmishing on the flank of the French, who were retiring under General Foy. On this day the SEVENTY-FOURTH had an opportunity of particularly distinguishing themselves. About eleven o'clock, the regiment

being in the valley, and the enemy moving in retreat 1813
parallel with the Allies along the mountain ridge to the left of the British, Lieut.-Colonel Trench obtained permission from Sir Thomas Picton to advance with the SEVENTY-FOURTH and cut off their rear. The regiment then ascended the ridge in view of the remainder of the division, which continued its advance up the valley; on approaching the summit, in passing through a wood, two companies, which were extended as skirmishers, were overpowered and driven back upon the main body, and the regiment was exposed to a most destructive fire, but continued its advance, without returning a shot, until it reached the upper skirt of the wood, close upon the flank of the enemy, and then at once opened its whole fire upon them. A column of fifteen or sixteen hundred men was separated from their main body, driven down the other side of the ridge, and a number taken prisoners; most of those who escaped were intercepted by the sixth division, which was further in advance on another line. After the SEVENTY-FOURTH had gained the ridge, another regiment from the third division was sent to support it, and pursued the remainder of the column until it had surrendered to the sixth division.

The regiment was highly complimented by the staff of the division for its conspicuous gallantry on this occasion, which was noticed as follows in Lord Wellington's despatch:—

"I cannot sufficiently applaud the conduct of all the "general officers, officers, and troops throughout these "operations, &c.

"The movement made by Sir Thomas Picton merited "my highest commendation; the latter officer co-ope- "rated in the attack of the mountain by detaching

1813 " troops to his left, in which Lieut.-Colonel the Hon. " R. Trench was wounded, but I hope not seriously."

The regiment sustained a loss of one officer, Captain Whitting, one serjeant, and four rank and file killed, and five officers, Lieut.-Colonel Honorable R. Trench, Captain (Brevet Major) Moore, and Lieutenants Pattison, Duncomb and Tew, four serjeants and thirty-six rank and file wounded, on this occasion.* Major Allen William Campbell,† of the SEVENTY-FOURTH, was also mortally wounded during the operations of this day while commanding a Portuguese battalion; he was gazetted to the brevet rank of Lieut.-Colonel for his distinguished conduct, but did not live to enjoy his promotion; he died of his wounds at Bilboa on the 10th of November 1813.

The regiment has received the Royal authority to bear on the regimental colour and appointments the word "PYRENEES," in commemoration of its services on this occasion.

The attack made by the French upon the British left on the 30th of July, was repulsed, and they retired during the night, but were closely pursued by the allies on the 31st, and after much hard fighting on that day, and on the 1st and 2nd of August, they were finally driven from the Spanish Pyrenees, over the Bidassoa into France, their attempt to relieve Pampeluna having entirely failed. Their losses in the different engagements from the 25th of July, amounted to above 15,000 men, killed, wounded, and prisoners. The SEVENTY-FOURTH continued to advance with the third division

* For non-commissioned officers and men, killed and wounded in the action near Pampeluna on 30th of July, 1813, *see* Appendix No. 6, page 138.

† Last surviving son of Lieut.-General Sir Alexander Campbell, *see* Appendix No. 2, page 128.

up the pass of Roncesvalles, and on the 1st of August encamped on a mountain a little to the left of it, but on the 5th was moved along the summits of the mountains on the left, to the pass of Maya; but shortly afterwards the third was relieved by the sixth division, and descended to Ariscan, in the valley of the Bastan, where it remained until the 5th of October. 1813

The fortress of *St. Sebastian* was taken by assault on the 31st of August, by the troops under Lieut.-General Sir Thomas Graham. Brevet Major Thomson, of the SEVENTY-FOURTH, who had been employed as an assistant engineer during the siege, received the brevet of Lieutenant-Colonel on the occasion. On the 6th of October, the third division, having been relieved by a Portuguese brigade, advanced up the pass of Zagaramurdi, and encamped on the summit of a mountain in front of the pass of Echalar; the left of the allied army passed the Bidassoa on the following day, driving the French from their strongly entrenched mountain position on the opposite side of the river.

The allied army was now organised in three grand divisions; the right, under Lieut.-General Sir Rowland Hill, occupied positions from the Roncesvalles pass to the Bastan; the centre, under Marshal Beresford, including the third, fourth, and seventh divisions, occupied the Echalar, Rhune, and Bayonette mountains; the left, under Lieut.-General Sir John Hope, extended from the Mandale mountain to the sea on the right bank of the Bidassoa.

The command of the third division devolved on Major-General Sir Charles Colville in the middle of October, Sir Thomas Picton having proceeded to England.

The SEVENTY-FOURTH remained in the same position, encamped on a bare mountain, until the 9th of November

1813 and suffered greatly from the constant exposure to cold and wet weather, the want of shelter and scarcity of provisions for men, and forage for animals. The piquets and night duties were likewise very harassing, and the dullness and monotony of such a position, wearisome to all ranks; the moment for the advance into France was therefore anxiously looked for. *Pampeluna* capitulated on the 31st of October. The attack upon the French position of the *Nivelle,* which had been ordered to take place on the occurrence of that event, was delayed by the continued heavy rains, and deep snow on the mountains, which rendered the movement of troops impossible until the 10th of November; on this day, the right, under Lieut.-General Sir Rowland Hill, was directed on the left of the French first line of entrenchments, between the Nivelle and Nive rivers, while the centre, under Marshal Beresford, turned the right of the French first line, and assaulted the redoubts and entrenchments on the left of the Nivelle. The third division, advancing from Zagaramurdi on the right of the centre attack, moved rapidly against the bridge of Amotz, where the enemy made a vigorous resistance, but were driven from it; the bridge and ground in front of it were taken possession of by the third division, which now attacked the left flank of the French centre, while the fourth and seventh divisions assailed them in front. Meanwhile the attacks of the second and sixth divisions on the right, and of the light division on the left, were everywhere successful. The French centre was driven in great confusion across the river, pursued by the skirmishers of the third division, which crossed at the bridge of Amotz. The allied troops then took possession of the heights on the right bank of the Nivelle, in the neighbourhood of St. Pé, and the French were compelled to abandon all the works which they had 1813 constructed with so much care and labour during the last three months, for the defence of the other parts of the position. On the 11th of November, the third and seventh divisions formed the right centre column in front of St. Pé, expecting to renew the attack, and the French advanced in order of battle, but drew back after a slight skirmish, breaking down the bridges on the Nive at Ustaritz, and on the 12th retired to close in front of their entrenched camp at Bayonne.

The weather had been fine and clear on the 10th, but heavy rain returned on the 11th and 12th of November, which rendered the fords of the Nive impassable, and the allied army was therefore stationary between the Nivelle and the Nive.

On the 18th of November the regiment was cantoned at Arrauntz, and in different farm-houses near the Nive, till the 12th of December.

The French had lost fifty-one pieces of artillery, and about 4300 officers and men killed, wounded, and prisoners, during the battle of the Nivelle. The loss of the allies was about 2700 officers and men.

The French army was now within the fortress and camp of *Bayonne*, with a line of entrenched out-posts extending from the Adour to the Nive, and from the Nive to the sea.

The regiment has received the Royal authority to bear on the regimental colour and appointments the word "NIVELLE," in commemoration of its services in this battle.

On the 9th of December the right of the army, under Lieut.-General Sir Rowland Hill, forced the passage of the *Nive* at Cambo, and the sixth division, under Marshal Beresford, at Ustaritz. The third division

1813 remained in possession of the bridge at Ustaritz, but had no share in the combats of the following days until the 13th, when the French having attacked the right between the Nive and Adour at St. Pierre, were repulsed by Sir Rowland Hill after a very severe battle, and the fourth, sixth, and two brigades of the third division, were moved across the Nive in support of the right.

The SEVENTY-FOURTH, after a very long day's march, arrived late at night on some heights near the village of Vieux Moguerre, on the Adour, from which another regiment had been driven in the morning; the SEVENTY-FOURTH afterwards remained cantoned in farm-houses between the Nive and Adour until the middle of Feb-
1814 ruary, 1814.

Lieut.-General Sir Thomas Picton had rejoined the army, and resumed the command of the third division in the end of December, 1813; and as many acts of outrage and plunder had been committed by the troops, on first entering France, he took an opportunity of publicly reprimanding some of the regiments of his division for such offences, when he thus addressed the SEVENTY-FOURTH:—"As for you, SEVENTY-FOURTH, I have "nothing to say against you, your conduct is gallant "in the field, and orderly in quarters." And, addressing Colonel Trench in front of the regiment, told him that he would write to the Colonel at home (General Sir Alexander Hope) his report of their good conduct. As Lieut.-General Picton was not habitually lavish of complimentary language, this public expression of the good opinion of so competent a judge was much valued by the regiment.

The French army under Marshal Soult having been weakened by the withdrawal of two divisions and others of his best troops, his plan of operations was changed,

and leaving a strong force in Bayonne, he moved the 1814
greater part of his troops to his left under his own command, to defend the country between the Adour and the Pyrenees, and to oppose the movement of the allied army to its right, and its advance across the Adour towards Bordeaux. The Marquis of Wellington determined, by a movement with part of his army to the right, to give occupation to the French, and thereby secure a passage across the Adour below Bayonne, and the complete investment of the place by the left of his army under Lieut.-General Sir John Hope.

The weather having improved, and the roads become practicable in the second week of February, the right of the army, consisting of the second and third divisions, with a division of Portuguese, and another of Spaniards, with cavalry and artillery, amounting altogether to about 20,000 men, was placed under Lieut.-General Sir Rowland Hill, and on the 14th of February commenced its march in two columns; the third division marched with the left column.

On the 15th there was an affair between the other column and the enemy at Garris, during which the Marquis of Wellington himself joined it and took the command, and the sixth and light divisions were brought up.

On the 24th of February, the French concentrated at *Orthes* on the river Gave de Pau; the third division was at the broken bridge of Bereaux, five miles lower down the river, on the 25th, having the sixth and seventh divisions (now arrived under Marshal Beresford) on its left, while the remainder of the force was assembled in front of Orthes. On the 26th the third division forded the river lower down, and a pontoon bridge was afterwards laid at Bereaux, by which the sixth and

1814 fourth divisions crossed on the morning of the 27th, at which time the third division was already posted with skirmishers thrown out close upon the left centre of the French position. The sixth division was placed on the right between the third division and the river, and the light division on its left in rear as a reserve. During the whole morning there had been occasional skirmishing by the third division, but the real attack commenced at nine o'clock by the third and sixth divisions on the French left centre, and the fourth and seventh divisions on their right, which last was intended to be the principal point of attack; but it having been found, after three hours' hard fighting, that the enemy were there too strongly posted, the Marquis of Wellington ordered an advance of the third and sixth divisions, with the fifty-second regiment, from the centre upon the left centre of the French position, which they carried and secured the victory; while Lord Hill, with the second division, had crossed the river above Orthes, and nearly cut off the only line of retreat open to the enemy, who then retired from the field, but without confusion, and constantly resisting the advance. The allies followed, keeping up an incessant fire and cannonade, but lost many men, particularly of the third division, which was the most strongly opposed; this continued until the French nearly reached the Luy de Bearn river, when their retreat became a flight, and they effected their escape by the fords and one bridge, which they destroyed, having lost 4000 men and six guns.

During the first advance, Lieut.-General Sir Thomas Picton particularly remarked to Major-General Brisbane the steady movement of his brigade; and the latter reported to him the notice he had taken of the gallantry of Serjeant-Major McPherson, of the SEVENTY-

FOURTH, upon which Sir Thomas Picton expressed to 1814
the Serjeant-Major his pleasure to hear such a good report of him, and on the following day, during a short halt on the march, desired Lieut.-Colonel Manners, who commanded the regiment in the absence of Lieut.-Colonel Trench, to write his recommendation, which he did on a drum-head; the Serjeant-Major was consequently promoted to a commission on the 31st of March following, and was afterwards a captain in the Regiment.*

The following Division Order was issued by Lieut.-General Sir Thomas Picton on the occasion of the battle of Orthes :—

" *Carzons, 4th March*, 1814.

" DIVISION ORDER.

" The Lieut.-General has great satisfaction in congratulating the division on the brilliant success of the attack made upon the enemy's position in the neighbourhood of Orthes, a very important part of which fell to the corps of the third division to execute.

" The Lieut.-General had, from his situation, a complete view of the whole operations of the division on that memorable day, and the respective regiments, British and Portuguese, are entitled to his entire approbation, &c."

The casualties in the regiment at the battle of Orthes were :—one serjeant and seven rank and file killed; and five officers, Captain Lyster, Lieut. Ewing, (mortally—died shortly afterwards,) Lieut. Ironside, Ensigns Shore and Luttrell, one serjeant, one drummer, and seventeen rank and file wounded.

---

* Captain McPherson is now a Staff Officer of pensioners at Paisley.

† For non-commissioned officers, drummers, and privates killed and wounded at Orthes, *see* Appendix No. 6, page 138.

1814 The regiment has received the Royal authority to bear on the regimental colour and appointments, the word "ORTHES," in commemoration of its services in this battle.

After the battle of Orthes, the French under Marshal Soult continued their retreat during the night to St. Sever, on the Adour, breaking down behind them all bridges over the streams which crossed their line of retreat, and also that over the Adour; they then turned to the right to Barcelonne, higher up the Adour, abandoning the direct road to Bordeaux.

On the 28th of February the allies advanced to St. Sever, but their operations were delayed by the necessity of repairing the bridges, especially as the smaller rivers and torrents were flooded by heavy rains.

The regiment was, with the rest of the third division, kept in movement, but not actively engaged with the enemy, until the 7th of March; it was then cantoned at Aire, on the left bank of the Adour, until the 13th. On the 14th it was moved, with the sixth division, to the river Lees, in support of Lieut.-General Sir Rowland Hill, who was threatened with a formidable attack, which however, did not take place. On the 18th of March the whole of the Allied army advanced up the Adour, occupying both sides of that river; the French falling back slowly before them. The third division was in the centre column, which, on the 19th, about mid-day, came up with a division of the French, drawn up on very defensible ground, among some vineyards in front of the town of *Vic Bigorre.* The Marquis of Wellington and Lieut.-General Sir Thomas Picton having reconnoitred the position, the third division was ordered to attack about two o'clock, and advanced, preceded by skirmishers; they drove the French before them without meeting so much opposition as was expected from the strength of the

position, and encamped in the evening about three 1814
miles beyond the town of Vic Bigorre.

The Marquis of Wellington stated in his despatch:—

"On the following day (the 19th) the enemy held a "strong rear-guard in the vineyards in front of the "town of Vic Bigorre; Lieut.-General Picton, with the "third division and Major-General Bock's brigade, made "a very handsome movement upon this rear-guard, "and drove them through the vineyards and town."

Two officers of the regiment, Lieut. Atkinson and Ensign Flood, were wounded in this affair.

The enemy retired in the night upon *Tarbes;* on the 20th of March, at daybreak, the allies advanced, the third, with the second division under Lord Hill, forming the right column, direct upon Tarbes. After some sharp fighting, in which the centre and left of the allies took the chief part, but in which the SEVENTY-FOURTH were also engaged, and lost some men, the right column crossed the Adour at Tarbes, and was encamped with the rest of the Allied army upon the Larret and Arroz rivers.

During the night Marshal Soult retreated towards *Toulouse*, followed on the 21st by the allies, who continued their advance, until on the 26th they arrived in presence of the French army, posted behind the Touch river, and covering Toulouse. This city, standing on the right bank of the river Garonne, above its junction with the great canal of Languedoc, is thus covered on three sides by water-courses. The suburb of St. Cyprien, on the left or western bank of the Garonne, communicates with the city by a bridge, but the city itself is accessible only from the south; and its strong though old-fashioned walls had been rendered more defensible by redoubts, and by an exterior line of entrenchments, on a strong and rugged range of heights about two miles in

1814 length, beyond the canal. On the 28th the enemy were driven within the suburb of St. Cyprien, and several attempts were made to attack them by crossing the Garonne above Toulouse. Operations were however impeded by the floods and rapidity of the river, until the 3rd of April, when the third, fourth, and sixth divisions, with three brigades of cavalry under Marshal Beresford, passed over by a pontoon bridge fifteen miles below Toulouse; but the crossing of the remainder of the army was again impeded by the rising of the river, which caused the removal of the bridges, until the 8th, when the Marquis of Wellington crossed and advanced within five miles of Toulouse; Sir Rowland Hill with two divisions remaining on the left bank.

The Marquis of Wellington then fixed his plan of attack on the French position, according to which, on the left of the Garonne Lieut.-General Sir Rowland Hill was to menace the suburb of St. Cyprien, while on the right of the river the third and light divisions were to menace the northern front, driving the enemy's outposts within the canal, from its junction with the Garonne to the commencement of the range of heights at the hill of Pugade. A Spanish division was to carry that hill, and the fourth and sixth divisions, under Marshal Beresford, to carry the heights beyond it. On the 10th of April, at about six o'clock in the morning, the battle commenced, and the different columns advanced according to order. The third division on the right, next the Garonne, drove in the outposts of the enemy for above three miles, as far as the bridge of Jumeaux on the canal; this bridge was defended by a strong palisaded *tête-de-pont*, too high to be forced without ladders, and approachable only along an open flat. Six companies of the SEVENTY-FOURTH (three under Brevet-Major Miller and three under

Captain McQueen) were ordered to attack this work, 1814
which they did in the most gallant style; but it was commanded from the opposite side of the canal, and was impregnable without artillery; the attacking party was therefore compelled to retire, after sustaining a most severe loss. The French then occupied the work in great force, and the continued efforts of the whole brigade could not dispossess them. The attack upon this work was unfortunately ordered by Lieut.-General Sir Thomas Picton, after the duty assigned to his division of driving in the outposts and menacing the enemy had been performed, although the impossibility of carrying the work without artillery had been represented to him.*

The Spanish attack upon the Pugade hill had meanwhile been repulsed, but after a long and severe contest, the fourth and sixth divisions carried the entrenched heights and works; the French then withdrew behind the canal, and thus ended the battle.

The casualties in the regiment at the battle of Toulouse were, four officers, Captains Thomas Andrews and William Tew, Lieut. Hamilton and Ensign John Parkinson, one serjeant, and thirty-two rank and file killed; and five officers, Brevet-Major Miller, Captain Donald McQueen, and Lieuts. Jason Hassard, William Graham, and E. J. Crabbe; four serjeants, and ninety-four rank and file wounded.†

The regiment has received the Royal authority to bear on the regimental colour and appointments, the word "TOULOUSE," in commemoration of its services in this battle.

Major-General Brisbane, (now General Sir Thomas

---

* Extract from Major Alves's Journal, *see* Appendix, No. 8, p. 141.

† For names of non-commissioned officers and privates killed and wounded at Toulouse, *see* Appendix No. 6, page 139.

1814 Brisbane, and Colonel of the thirty-fourth regiment,) commanded the brigade, and was wounded.

The French lost five generals, and about three thousand officers and men, and the Allies four generals and about four thousand officers and men, including two thousand Spaniards killed and wounded in this hard-fought, but as it proved, unnecessary battle.

On the 11th of April the renewal of the attack was delayed by the want of ammunition, and the French abandoned the city during the night, retiring to the southward upon Carcassonne. On the 12th the Allies entered Toulouse in triumph; in the afternoon of the same day intelligence arrived of the abdication of Napoleon and the termination of the war. Had not the officers conveying this intelligence been detained on their journey by the police, the battle of Toulouse, and the sacrifice of many valuable lives, would have been prevented.

The regiment remained in Toulouse until the 24th, when it marched down the Garonne to Grenade and was cantoned there, until, on the 1st of June, it marched for Blanquefort, near Bordeaux, where it arrived and was encamped on the 13th. On the 14th of June, the Duke of Wellington took leave of his Peninsular army in a well-known general order.*

The SEVENTY-FOURTH marched on the 26th of June to the village of Chateau Margaux, where the regiment was cantoned, until on the 4th of July it marched in the morning to *Pauillac*, and was conveyed in a transport to Verdun roads, where it was transferred with part of the 60th regiment to His Majesty's ship "Clarence" of 74 guns, and on the 25th of July disembarked at Cove, and marched to Cork.

---

* *See* Appendix No. 9, page 142.

The SEVENTY-FOURTH, although only a single battalion regiment, had thus remained effective in the field, and maintained its place in the fighting division during the whole period from its leaving Lisbon to join the army on the 27th of February, 1810, until its embarkation at *Pauillac* on the 4th of July, 1814. 1814

The record of its services during these eventful years, will be sufficient to prove how well the corps maintained the high character it had at first acquired in the East Indies, and how well it earned the distinction, since conferred upon it, of bearing the word "PENINSULA" on the regimental colour and appointments.

In consideration of the meritorious conduct of the non-commissioned officers and men of the regiment during the war, Colonel Trench applied to the Commander-in-Chief to authorise those most distinguished among them to wear silver medals in commemoration of their services. The sanction of the Commander-in-Chief was conveyed to Colonel Trench in a letter from the Adjutant-General, bearing date "Horse Guards, 30th June, 1814."

Medals were accordingly granted to the deserving survivors of the campaigns, who were divided into three classes; first class, men who had served in eight or nine general actions; second class, in six or seven general actions; third class, in four or five general actions.

Shortly after its arrival in Ireland, the regiment marched from Cork to Galway.

In January, 1815, it was notified to Colonel Trench that His Royal Highness the Prince Regent had been pleased to confer upon him the distinction of a Knight Commander of the Order of the Bath, in consideration of his eminent services while in command of the SEVENTY-FOURTH regiment. Major and Brevet Lieut.-Colonel Manners was appointed a Companion of the Order at the same time. 1815

1817 In the month of June, the regiment was suddenly ordered from Galway to Cork, for the purpose of embarking on service in Belgium, but before it reached Cork, news had been received of the termination of the war by the crowning victory of Waterloo; the regiment was therefore sent to Limerick, and the head-quarters immediately moved to Rathkeale, being there stationed, with various detachments throughout the country, which was then in a very disturbed state. In the
1816 month of March, 1816, the detachments were relieved and marched to Dublin, where the regiment was con-
1817 centrated until July, 1817, when it was removed to the north of Ireland, and the head-quarters were stationed at Strabane, with various detachments.*

1818 On the 16th of February, 1818, the regiment marched from Strabane to Fermoy, being under orders to embark for Colonial Service in North America.

At Fermoy, on the 6th of April, new colours were presented to the corps. The old ones, which had been received in 1802, and carried in so many victorious fields, were burned, and the ashes deposited in the lid of a gold sarcophagus snuff-box, inlaid with part of the wood of the colour staves, on which the following inscription was engraved:—"This box, composed of the "old standards of the SEVENTY-FOURTH regiment, was "formed as a tribute of respect to the memory of those "who fell, and of esteem for those who survived the "many glorious and arduous services on which they "were always victoriously carried, during a period of "sixteen years in India, the Peninsula, and France. "They were presented to the regiment at Wallajahbad "in 1802, and the shattered remains were burned at "Fermoy on the 6th of April, 1818." This box has

* For establishment of the regiment in 1818, *see* Appendix No. 5, page 133.

been ever since carefully preserved by the officers as a 1818
sacred relique.

The regiment was marched from Fermoy to Cork, embarked on board five transports at Cove on the 9th, and sailed for Halifax, Nova Scotia, on the 13th of May, leaving one depôt company, which was sent to the Isle of Wight.

On arrival at Halifax, three companies under a Field Officer, were sent to St. John's, Newfoundland; the remainder proceeded to St. John's, New Brunswick, and landed on the 8th of July. Two companies remained stationed there; but the head-quarters and five companies proceeded to Frederickton.

In the end of the year 1818, the establishment of the regiment was reduced to ten companies of sixty-five rank and file.

In the month of August, 1821, it was again reduced 1821
to eight companies of seventy-two rank and file.

Nothing worthy of notice occurred to vary the usual routine of peaceful colonial service, and the regiment and detachments remained at the same stations until
the end of July, 1823, when it embarked at St. John's 1823
for Halifax, Nova Scotia, where the whole was brought together in the month of September.

On the 21st of May, 1825, a company was embarked 1825
for Bermuda, and two more followed on the 11th of July, but the whole returned to Halifax in the month of October.

In the month of August, 1825, the establishment was augmented to ten companies; six service companies of eighty-six rank and file, and four depôt companies of fifty-six rank and file. The non-commissioned officers and staff for the formation of a four-company depôt, were sent to England on the commencement of the new system.

1828 On the 9th of August, 1828, three divisions of the regiment embarked for Bermuda, where they arrived on the 24th; the head-quarters and remainder of the regiment embarked on the 24th, and landed at Bermuda on the 31st of August.

1829 In December, 1829, the service companies were ordered home from Bermuda, and the head-quarters and three companies, under Lieut.-Colonel Mein, embarked on the 24th, sailed on the 27th of December, 1829,
1830 and arrived at Cork on the 10th of February, 1830; the remaining three companies, under Major Hutchinson, embarked on the 14th of January, and arrived at Cork on the 27th of February, 1830.

The depôt companies had landed at Cork, from England, on the 18th of August, 1829, and were united with the service companies on their arrival; the regiment remained at Cork from February until August, 1830, when it marched to Limerick, and was there stationed.

1831 On the 23rd of February, 1831, three companies of two hundred men, under Major Crabbe, marched from Limerick to Ennis; on the 18th of March one hundred and twenty men proceeded to the same place, and during the remainder of the month and beginning of April, the rest of the regiment, excepting the staff and one company, marched to various stations in the county of Clare, where the corps was employed for several months on constant active duty in consequence of the disturbances and outrages existing in the country.

In the month of October, 1831, the regiment was
1832 removed to Templemore; in September, 1832, to Kil-
1833
1834 kenny; in May, 1833, to Dublin; in April, 1834, to Newry; and in July to Belfast; where, in the beginning of

September, an order was received to form a four-company 1834
depôt, and for the six service companies to embark for Barbadoes. The first division, consisting of three companies under Major McQueen, was accordingly conveyed by steamers from Belfast on the 24th, arriving at Kingston harbour on the following day, and embarked, under Major Mannin, on the 1st of October (Major McQueen having retired from the service), on board of the "Amity" transport for Barbadoes, where it arrived on the 19th of November, but, being put in quarantine, did not disembark until the 9th of December. The head-quarter division, consisting of the three remaining companies, under Lieutenant-Colonel Mein, was conveyed by steamer from Belfast on the 1st, and arrived at Kingston on the 2nd of October, embarked on board of the "Lord Wellington" transport on the 16th of October, reached Barbadoes on the 29th of November, and was then ordered to proceed to the island of Grenada, where it disembarked on the 6th of December, 1834. The regiment remained thus stationed, divided into two wings,
until November 1835, when, in obedience to a General 1835
Order, dated Barbadoes, 23rd October, the left wing embarked at Barbadoes on the 3rd, and landed at Antigua on the 5th of November. The head-quarters and right wing embarked at Grenada on the 13th, and landed at Antigua on the 17th of November. The regiment remained at Antigua until the 5th of February,
ruary, 1837, when it embarked for Dominica and St. 1837
Lucia; three companies landed at Dominica on the 9th, and the remaining three companies and head-quarters arrived at St. Lucia on the 12th of February. An order was subsequently received for the head-quarters to move to St. Vincent, in consequence of which one company embarked at Dominica on the 30th of May,

1837 and arrived at St. Lucia on the 2nd of June, where the head-quarters and another company were taken on board the same transport, and arrived at St. Vincent on the 12th of June.

1838 In April, 1838, an order was received for the regiment to return to St. Lucia, and for two companies to be sent to Barbadoes. Accordingly the head-quarters and all at St. Vincent embarked on the 28th of April; the head-quarters landed at St. Lucia on the 5th of May, and the two companies from St. Vincent proceeded to Barbadoes.

1839 In January, 1839, the head-quarters and two companies were removed from St. Lucia to Barbadoes, but were again moved to Trinidad in the following month, where the regiment remained, with one company at
1840 Tobago, until June, 1840, when it was moved to Barbadoes, and the whole of the service companies were united there in the following month, for the first time since their arrival in the West Indies. During the time the regiment was stationed at Trinidad, from November, 1839, it was attacked by fever and dysentery, which caused great mortality, and fever continued prevalent in the regiment until its removal to Barbadoes; with this exception the SEVENTY-FOURTH regiment remained remarkably healthy during the whole of its service in the West Indies.

1841 On the 1st of May, 1841, the regiment sailed from Barbadoes for Canada, and on the 29th arrived at Quebec, whence it was immediately sent on to Montreal,
1842 and remained there until May, 1842, when it moved to La Prairie. After occupying that station for two
1844 years the regiment was moved, in May, 1844, to Quebec, where it remained until it embarked, in three divisions, for Halifax, Nova Scotia, in September, and was

united there in the following month. The term of its 1844
colonial service being now ended, the regiment, under the command of Lieutenant-Colonel Crabbe, was embarked
at Halifax for England on the 4th of March, 1845, 1845
on board of Her Majesty's troop ship "Resistance;" arrived off Deal on the 27th, disembarked at Deal on the 29th of March, and proceeded to Canterbury, where the depôt was then stationed, and was amalgamated with the service companies immediately on their arrival.

Shortly after its return from America, Lieutenant-Colonel Crabbe, commanding the regiment, submitted to the Commander-in-Chief, through the Colonel (Lieutenant-General Sir Phineas Riall), the earnest desire of the officers and men to be permitted to resume the national garb and designation of a Highland regiment, under which the SEVENTY-FOURTH had been originally embodied.

The Lieutenant-Colonel having himself first joined the regiment as a Highland corps in the year 1807, and having served with it continuously during the intervening period, knew by his own experience, and was able to certify to the Commander-in-Chief, how powerfully and favourably its character had been influenced by its original organization; and also that throughout the varied services and changes of so many years, a strong national feeling, and a connexion with Scotland by recruiting, had been constantly maintained. Various considerations, however, induced an application for permission to modify the original dress of kilt and feathered bonnet, and with the resumed designation of a Highland corps, to adopt the trews and bonnet as established for the seventy-first regiment.

His Grace the Duke of Wellington was pleased to return a favourable answer to the application, in such

1845 terms as to render his consent doubly gratifying to the corps, causing it to be intimated to the Colonel, by a letter from the Adjutant-General, bearing date "Horse Guards, 13th August, 1845,"* that he would recommend to Her Majesty that the SEVENTY-FOURTH regiment should be permitted to resume the appellation of a Highland regiment, and to be clothed "accordingly in compliment to the services of that regiment so well known to His Grace in India and in Europe."

Subsequently, in the Gazette of the 14th November, 1845, the following announcement was published:—

"*War Office, 8th November*, 1845.

"MEMORANDUM.—Her Majesty has been graciously "pleased to approve of the SEVENTY-FOURTH foot "resuming the appellation of the SEVENTY-FOURTH "(Highland) regiment of foot, and of its being clothed "accordingly; that is, to wear the tartan trews instead "of the Oxford mixture; plaid cap instead of the "black chaco; and the plaid scarf as worn by the "seventy-first regiment.

"The alteration of the dress is to take place on the "next issue of clothing, on the 1st of April, 1846."

The national designation of the regiment was of course immediately resumed, and the recruiting has been since carried on solely in Scotland with uniform success.

The alteration of the regimental uniform, as sanctioned by Her Majesty, was effected at the date above-mentioned.

The regiment remained at Canterbury from the 29th of March to the 29th of August, 1845, when it proceeded to Gosport.

---

* *See* Appendix No. 11, page 144.

On the 3rd of January, 1846, the regiment moved 1846
to Portsmouth, whence, in the month of August, it was ordered to Scotland.

A detachment of two companies for Dundee, and one for Perth, embarked on board the "Athol" troop ship on the 22nd of August, and landed at Dundee on the 3rd of September.

A detachment of one field officer and two companies for Paisley embarked on the 9th of September, on board Her Majesty's steamer "Scourge," and landed at Leith on the 12th.

The head-quarters, with two field officers and three companies, embarked on board of Her Majesty's steamer "Gladiator" on the 12th of September, and landed at Aberdeen on the 15th.

A detachment of one company for Stirling and Dunfermline, and one for Paisley, embarked on the 23rd of September, on board Her Majesty's steamer "Scourge," and landed at Leith on the 25th.

The regiment remained at Aberdeen with the before-mentioned detachments until the 25th of November, when it was moved by steamer to Granton pier, landed there on the following day, and proceeded by railway to Glasgow, where it was joined by the detachments from Dundee, Perth, Stirling, and Dunfermline.

In July, 1847, the regiment was ordered to Ireland, 1847
and embarked at Glasgow, the first division on the 3rd of July, and the head-quarter division on the 8th, on board of Her Majesty's steamer "Birkenhead," landing at Belfast on the following days. It remained stationed there until the month of December, when it was moved to Dublin, and the head-quarters arrived in Richmond Barracks, Dublin, on the 16th of December, 1847, but remained with five companies on de-

1848 tachment until the end of March, 1848, when the regiment was brought together, and was in the end of June moved into the Castle and Ship-street barracks.

In consequence of the disturbed state of the country, and an apprehended insurrectionary movement in the county of Tipperary, the SEVENTY-FOURTH received orders on the evening of the 28th of July to proceed on the following morning to that county, to be employed as part of a moveable column under Major-General McDonald, leaving one company as a depôt, with recruits and sick men, at the Ship-street barracks, Dublin.

The regiment was accordingly, on the morning of the 29th of July, conveyed with a half-battery of artillery, a detachment of sappers, and three companies of the 60th rifles, by railway to Thurles, where it received camp equipage, was joined by a squadron of cavalry, and proceeded to Ballingarry and Killenaule, and encamped.

The seventy-fifth and eighty-fifth regiments afterwards joined the column, and with the SEVENTY-FOURTH were kept under canvas, and occasionally moved about to different encampments in the neighbourhood of Thurles and Ballingarry during the month of August.

The contemptible attempt at rebellion was, however, put down without anything more than the demonstration of an armed force, and the regiment returned to Dublin in the beginning of September, having found nothing to contend with, excepting the discomfort of almost continual rain during the period of its field employment: on its return to Dublin it was quartered in the Royal barracks, until the month of December, when it proceeded to Limerick.

The regiment still forms a part of the garrison of

Madeley lith. 3 Wellington St. Strand

PIPER. OFFICER. PRIVATE.

SEVENTY FOURTH HIGHLANDERS.

For Cannon's Military Records.

Limerick, and retains the hope of obtaining a more 1850
active field for the display of its energies, and of giving to a future historian of the SEVENTY-FOURTH Highlanders, the duty of recording achievements worthy of a place beside those of the victors of *Assaye*, and of the stormers of *Badajoz*.

1850

SUCCESSION OF COLONELS

OF

THE SEVENTY-FOURTH REGIMENT,

(HIGHLANDERS).

Sir Archibald Campbell, K.B.,

Appointed 12*th October*, 1787.

Major-General Sir Archibald Campbell, who raised the Seventy-fourth regiment in the year 1787, was appointed its first Colonel, and a few years after his decease, which occurred in 1791, a monument was erected to his memory in Westminster Abbey, which records his services to his King and Country, and a copy of the inscription thereon is inserted at page 125.

Charles O'Hara,

Appointed 1*st April*, 1791.

Charles O'Hara was appointed cornet in the third dragoons in December, 1752, and in 1756 he was promoted to lieutenant and captain in the second foot guards. He served in Portugal in 1762, and performed the duties of quartermaster-general to the army under Lieut.-General the Earl of Loudoun. In 1769 he was promoted to the rank of captain and lieut.-colonel; and he served with his regiment in North America. In the autumn of 1781 he was promoted to the rank of major-general. He commanded the brigade of foot guards under Lieut.-General the Earl Cornwallis, in Virginia; distinguished himself at the passage of the Catawba river, on the 1st of February, 1781; and was wounded at the battle of Guildford on the 15th of March. In 1782 he was nominated to the colonelcy of the twenty-second regiment; was removed to the SEVENTY-FOURTH HIGHLANDERS in 1791, and was advanced to the rank of lieut.-general in 1793. He commanded the British troops at Toulon, and was wounded and taken prisoner in an action with the French republican troops on the 30th of November, 1793. His services were rewarded with the appointment of Governor of Gibraltar, and in 1798 he was promoted to the rank of general. It is recorded that he possessed a happy combination of talents; was a brave and enterprising soldier, a strict disciplinarian, and a polite and accomplished gentleman. He died at Gibraltar on the 21st of February, 1802.

JOHN LORD HUTCHINSON, K.B.,

Appointed 21st March, 1802.

THE HONORABLE JOHN HELY HUTCHINSON entered the army in January, 1774, as cornet in the eighteenth light dragoons, and in October, 1776, he was promoted captain of a company in the sixty-seventh regiment: in 1777 he was elected a Member of Parliament for Cork. On the 21st September, 1781, he was advanced to the rank of major in the seventy-seventh, or Athol Highlanders, in which corps he rose to the rank of lieut.-colonel in 1783; but his regiment was disbanded on the termination of the American war. Having previously studied tactics at Strasburg, he again visited the Continent, and acquired additional information on military subjects. Soon after the commencement of the French revolutionary war, he returned to the United Kingdom; was promoted to the rank of colonel on the 1st of March, 1794; and, taking great interest in raising the ninety-fourth regiment, he was appointed colonel of that corps in October, which was reduced in 1795. He served two campaigns in Flanders, as extra aid-de-camp to lieut.-general Sir Ralph Abercromby. He was promoted to the rank of major-general in 1796; and serving in Ireland during the rebellion in 1798, he was second in command at the action at Castlebar. He also served in the expedition to Holland in 1799, and honorable mention is made of his gallant conduct in the public despatches. Having given proof of his capabilities as a General Officer, he was nominated second in command in the expedition to Egypt, under Lieut.-General Sir Ralph Abercromby; and after the death of that officer from wounds received in the action of the 21st of March, the command of the troops devolved on Major-General Hutchinson, who found himself suddenly placed at the head of the army under circumstances of a peculiarly difficult character. In the subsequent operations in Egypt he evinced talent and energy, sustaining the honour of his Sovereign, promoting the glory of his country, and forcing the French "Army of the East" to evacuate Egypt. For his services in this enterprise he twice received the thanks of both Houses of Parliament; he gained the approbation of his Sovereign; was nominated a Knight of the Bath; received the Order of the Crescent from the Grand Seignior; was elevated to the peerage by the title of BARON HUTCHINSON OF ALEXANDRIA and of Knocklofty, in the county of Tipperary; and received an important addition to his income. He was also nominated Governor of Stirling Castle; and was appointed by His Majesty, Colonel of the SEVENTY-FOURTH regiment on the 21st of March, 1802. In 1803 his Lordship was promoted to the rank of Lieut.-General.

The subsequent services of Lord Hutchinson were of a diplomatic character: in November, 1806, he proceeded on an extraordinary mission to the Prussian and Russian armies; and he afterwards proceeded to the Court of St. Petersburg. In 1806 he was nominated to the colonelcy of the fifty-seventh regiment, and was removed in 1811 to the eighteenth Royal Irish regiment. In 1813 he was promoted to the rank of General. On the decease of his brother, in 1825, he succeeded to the title of EARL OF DONOUGHMORE. He died on the 6th of July, 1832.

SIR JOHN STUART, K.B., COUNT OF MAIDA,

Appointed 8th September, 1806.

JOHN STUART obtained a commission of ensign in the Third Foot Guards in 1779, and proceeding to North America, received a dangerous wound, while serving under Earl Cornwallis, in Carolina. On the breaking out of the war of the French revolution in 1793, he accompanied his regiment to Flanders, and was soon afterwards promoted to captain and lieut.-colonel: he was engaged in numerous services, and eventually commanded one of the battalions of foot guards serving under His Royal Highness the Duke of York. In 1796 he was promoted to the rank of colonel. He served as brigadier-general in Portugal; also in the successful expedition against Minorca, where he obtained the command of a regiment raised on the island, afterwards the Queen's German Regiment, which was numbered, on the 6th of June, 1808, the ninety-seventh regiment, and was disbanded on the 10th of December, 1818.

From Minorca he proceeded with the expedition to Egypt, under Lieut.-General Sir Ralph Abercromby, and evinced talent and enterprise at the head of a foreign brigade, at the battle of Alexandria, on the 21st of March, 1801; the French Invincible standard was one of the trophies acquired by the Queen's German Regiment. At the termination of the campaign in Egypt, he returned to England, from whence he proceeded on a political mission to Constantinople; and afterwards assumed the command of the British troops at Alexandria; his conduct during the period that Egypt was the scene of civil war between the Turks and Mamelukes, procured him the approbation of his Sovereign; and he was permitted to receive the Order of the Crescent from the Grand Seignior. On the 29th of April, 1802, he was promoted to the rank of major-general; and in 1804 and 1805 he commanded a brigade on the coast of Kent, in readiness to repel the menaced French invasion. He afterwards accompanied Lieut.-General Sir James Craig with the expedition to Naples, and was left in command of the British troops on the island of Sicily. The French assembled a force in Calabria, for the invasion of Sicily, and Major-General Stuart formed the design of cutting off the French division under General Regnier; the result was the BATTLE OF MAIDA, where, on the 4th of July 1806, a victory was gained which reflected great credit on Major-General Stuart, and lustre on the British arms. The British Minister at Palermo stated, in an official communication—"There is not to be found in the annals of military transactions an enterprise prepared with more deliberate reflection, or executed with greater decision, promptitude, and success, than the late invasion of Calabria by Sir John Stuart. I trust, therefore, you will not think me presumptuous, for venturing to add my testimony of the high sense entertained by this Court, of the merits of the British General, and of his gallant army, who on the fertile plains of Maida, have added new trophies to those which the same troops had formerly earned from the same enemy, on the sandy regions of Egypt." For his conduct on this occasion, Major-General Stuart received the thanks of Parliament with the vote of a thousand pounds a year for life, the approbation of his Sovereign, and the dignity of Knight of the Bath; he was created COUNT OF MAIDA by the King of the Two Sicilies; and the city of London voted him their freedom and a sword; and on the 8th of September, 1806, His Majesty King George III., conferred on him the colonelcy of the SEVENTY-FOURTH regiment. He was advanced to the rank of lieut.-general on the 25th April, 1808; and on the 29th December of the following year His Majesty King George III. conferred on him the colonelcy of the twentieth regiment. He again distinguished himself in defeating the designs of Marshal Murat, on whom Napoleon had conferred the kingdom of Naples, and who made extensive preparations for the invasion of Sicily; but sustained a decisive repulse in 1810, when a French standard was captured; and the COUNT OF MAIDA was rewarded with the Order of St. Gennaro. Lieut.-General Sir John Stuart, after his return to England, was appointed, on the 10th of June, 1813, to the command of the western district of Great Britain. He died in 1815.

THE HONORABLE SIR ALEXANDER HOPE, G.C.B.

Appointed 29*th December* 1809.

THE HONORABLE ALEXANDER HOPE entered the army as ensign in the sixty-third regiment, on the 6th of March, 1786, and after a service of upwards of thirteen years he was promoted to the lieutenant-colonelcy of the fourteenth Foot, on the 27th of August, 1794. He commanded the regiment during its retreat through Holland, and in the attack of the French post at Gueldermalsen, on the 8th of January, 1795, he received a wound in the shoulder, which deprived him of the use of his right arm. He was appointed governor of Tynemouth and Clifford's fort, in 1797; lieutenant-governor of Edinburgh Castle, in 1798; and deputy adjutant-general to the expedition to Holland, in 1799. He was promoted to the rank of colonel in the army, on the 1st of January, 1800; and to the colonelcy of the Fifth West India Regiment, on the 30th of October, 1806. In April, 1808, he was further promoted to the rank of major-general, and on the 29th of December 1809, was appointed colonel of the SEVENTY-FOURTH regiment. In April, 1813, he was removed to the colonelcy of the forty-seventh regiment; and in June of the same year, he was advanced to the rank of lieutenant-general. He obtained the rank of general on the 22nd of July, 1830; and the colonelcy of the fourteenth regiment, in 1835. He was nominated a Knight Grand Cross of the Honorable Order of the Bath, and he was also appointed lieutenant-governor of the Royal Hospital of Chelsea: he died on the 19th of May, 1837.

JAMES MONTGOMERIE,

Appointed 26*th April*, 1813.

THIS Officer was appointed ensign in the fifty-first regiment, on the 13th of September, 1773; he joined at Minorca in the beginning of 1774; and in 1775 exchanged into the thirteenth foot. In the following year he returned with the regiment to England, and in 1779 was promoted to a lieutenancy. In February, 1780, he was promoted to a company in the late ninety-third regiment, and sailed with an expedition to the West Indies. Soon after arriving at Jamaica, the ninety-third regiment was drafted and sent home: Captain Montgomerie remained in that island on the staff, as major of brigade to General Garth, and at the end of the year 1781 returned to Europe. On the reduction of the ninety-third regiment at the peace of 1783, this officer was removed to the tenth foot, and joined in Jamaica in 1786; in 1790 he was sent to England on the recruiting service, and in February, 1793, he rejoined his regiment and continued with it until 1794. On arriving in England, he was appointed major of brigade on the Home Staff under Major-General Bruce's command; in March 1794, he received the brevet rank of major, and in May, 1795, was appointed lieutenant-colonel of the sixth West India regiment; he sailed with the officers to Martinique in order to raise that corps, but not succeeding, he volunteered his services in the expedition under General Sir Ralph Abercromby in 1796, and was appointed to command the troops at

St. Kitts, where he remained until 1798, when he exchanged into the forty-fifth regiment, which he joined at Dominica; but ill health shortly afterwards compelled him to return to England. He was appointed colonel by brevet on the 29th of April, 1802; and in 1804 he was appointed lieutenant-colonel in the sixty-fourth regiment. In February of the latter year he was appointed brigadier-general in the West Indies. He sailed in March with General Sir William Myers, commander of the forces, and was selected by the government to hold the civil and military command at Tobago. In 1805 he was removed to the colonies of Demerara and Berbice, where he remained until November, 1808, during the greater part of which time he acted as governor of those colonies. He was then removed by General Sir George Beckwith to Dominica, and in 1809 he returned to England. On the 25th of October, 1809, he received the rank of major-general, and on the 26th of April, 1813, was appointed by the Prince Regent, in the name and behalf of His Majesty, to the colonelcy of the SEVENTY-FOURTH regiment. On the 4th of June, 1814, he was advanced to the rank of lieutenant-general. His Majesty King George the Fourth, appointed Lieut.-General Montgomerie to be colonel of the thirtieth regiment, on the 13th of June, 1823, which he retained until his decease in the year 1829.

THE HONORABLE SIR CHARLES COLVILLE, G.C.B., G.C.H.,

Appointed 13th June, 1823.

On the 26th of December 1781, this officer was appointed ensign in the twenty-eighth regiment, which he joined in Ireland on the 13th of June, 1787; in September, 1787, he was promoted lieutenant, and on the 24th of January, 1791, was promoted to an independent company, and on the 26th of May following was appointed to the thirteenth regiment. Captain Colville joined the thirteenth regiment at Jamaica in December, 1791; he accompanied the expedition to St. Domingo in September, 1793, and was present at most of the attacks and skirmishes, between that time and June, 1795, when he returned to England. On the 1st of September, 1795, he was promoted to the rank of major in the thirteenth, and on the 26th of August, 1796, to that of lieut.-colonel. He served with the thirteenth in Ireland during the rebellion; in the expedition to Ferrol in 1800; and to Egypt in 1801. Lieut.-Colonel Colville was present in the action on landing on the 8th of March, and in those of the 13th and 21st of that month; and was subsequently employed in the investment of Alexandria, and continued in Egypt until March 1802. In August, 1803, he joined his regiment at Gibraltar, and did duty there until May, 1805. On the 1st of January, 1805, he received the brevet rank of colonel; in February, 1808, Colonel Colville accompanied his regiment to Bermuda; on the 25th of December, 1809, he was appointed brigadier-general, and was employed in the command of the second brigade of General Sir George Prevost's division of the army, in the investment and siege of Fort Dessaix, and in the absence of Major-General Maitland, to the command of the garrison of Grenada. On the 25th of July, 1810, he was advanced to the rank of major-general, and was appointed to the colonelcy of the fifth garrison battalion on the 10th of October, 1812, and he subsequently served on the staff of the Peninsula. On the 29th of April, 1815, he was appointed colonel of the ninety-fourth regiment (late Scots Brigade), which was disbanded on the 24th of December, 1818; and on the 12th of August, 1819, he was promoted lieut.-general. He was nominated a Knight Commander of the Order of the Bath for his distinguished services, and His Majesty King George the Fourth, conferred on him the colonelcy of the SEVENTY-FOURTH regiment on the 13th of June, 1823. In January, 1828, lieut.-general the Honorable Sir Charles Colville was appointed governor of the Mauritius, and also to the command of the troops in that island, where he remained until January, 1833. On the 12th of December, 1834, he was removed to the fourteenth regiment of foot; and on the 25th of March, 1835, he was appointed colonel of the fifth regiment of foot, or Northumberland Fusiliers, and on the 10th of January, 1837, was advanced to the rank of general. General the Honorable Sir Charles Colville, G.C.B. G.C.H. died on the 27th of March, 1843.

SIR JAMES CAMPBELL, K.C.B., K.C.H.,

Appoin ed 12th December, 1834.

THIS Officer commenced his military career as ensign in the first or royal regiment of foot, his commission being dated

30th of March, 1791. He was promoted to a lieutenancy in the regiment on the 20th of March, 1794; was placed on half-pay in January, 1795, and in December, 1797, he was gazetted to a company in the forty-second royal Highland regiment. In June, 1799, he was promoted to the rank of major in the Argyle Fencibles, and was removed to the ninety-fourth regiment on the 7th of April, 1802. He was promoted to the rank of lieut.-colonel in the ninety-fourth regiment, on the 27th of September, 1804. On the 4th of June, 1813, he received the brevet rank of colonel; and on the 12th of August, 1819, he was advanced to the rank of major-general. On the 3rd of December, 1822, His Majesty King George the Fourth nominated him a Knight Commander of the most honourable Order of the Bath, and King William the Fourth conferred on him the colonelcy of the ninety-fourth regiment on the 13th of April, 1831, from which he was removed to the SEVENTY-FOURTH regiment on the 12th of December, 1834. Major-General Sir James Campbell died at Paris, on the 6th of May, 1835.

SIR PHINEAS RIALL, K.C.H.,

Appointed 20th May, 1835.
Removed to the Fifteenth Regiment of Foot on the 24th April, 1846.

SIR ALEXANDER CAMERON, K.C.B.,

Appointed 24th April, 1846.

Succession of Lieutenant-Colonels of the Seventy-fourth Regiment, (Highlanders).

NAMES.	Date of Appointment.	Date of Removal.	REMARKS.
Gordon Forbes	12 Oct. 1787	14 Dec. 1788	Died.
Hamilton Maxwell . . .	15 Dec. 1788	8 June 1794	Died.
Marlborough Parsons Sterling	9 June 1794	4 Dec. 1795	Died.
Alexander Ross	5 Dec. 1795	3 Dec. 1796	Died.
Robert Shawe	1 Sept. 1795	24 Dec. 1798	Exchanged to 12th Foot.
Alexander Campbell . . .	4 Dec. 1796	25 July 1810	Promoted Major-General.
William Harness	24 Dec. 1798	7 June 1800	Returned to 18th Foot by General Orders of the 7th June, 1800.
Robert Shawe	7 June 1800	1 Dec. 1803	Resumed his situation in the Regiment by General Orders of the 7th June, 1800; retired 1st Dec. 1803.
Samuel Swinton	1 Dec. 1803	13 May 1805	Promoted in 75th Regiment.
Malcolm McPherson . . .	14 May 1807	21 Sept. 1809	Exchanged to Inspecting Field Officer, Canada.
Hon. Robert Le Poer Trench	21 Sept. 1809	14 Mar. 1823	Died.
John Alexander Mein. . .	20 Mar. 1823	5 Nov. 1841	Died.
Eyre John Crabbe . . .	6 Nov. 1841	1 May 1846	Retired on Full-pay.
William White Crawley . .	1 May 1846	10 July 1846	Retired.
John Fordyce	10 July 1846	..	..

Succession of Majors of the Seventy-fourth Regiment (Highlanders).

NAMES.	Date of Appointment.	Date of Removal.	REMARKS.
Francis Skelly . . .	5 Nov. 1788	30 Nov. 1793	Died.
Robert Shawe. . . .	1 Dec. 1793	28 Mar. 1795	Exchanged to 76th Foot.
Alexander Ross . . .	28 Mar. 1795	4 Dec. 1795	Promoted Lieut.-Colonel.
Alexander Campbell .	25 Dec. 1795	4 Dec. 1796	Promoted Lieut.-Colonel.
William Wallace . .	2 Sept. 1795	22 Nov. 1803	Promoted in the 19th Dragoons.
William Douglas . .	4 Dec. 1796	17 May 1799	Promoted in 85th Foot.
Samuel Swinton . . .	17 May 1799	1 Dec. 1803	Promoted Lieut.-Colonel.
James Robertson . . .	22 Nov. 1803	14 Nov. 1804	Retired.
Francis R. West . . .	1 Dec. 1803	15 Nov. 1804	Retired.
Malcolm McPherson. .	14 Nov. 1804	13 May 1807	Promoted Lieut-Colonel.
Hon. McDonnell Murray	15 Nov. 1804	10 Mar. 1808	Died.
Edward Broughton . .	14 May 1807	4 Apr. 1810	Retired.
Russell Manners* . .	11 Mar. 1808	18 Apr. 1822	Retired.
Allen William Campbell†	5 Apr. 1810	10 Nov. 1813	Died of wounds.
John Alexander Mein .	11 Nov. 1813	20 Mar. 1823	Promoted Lieut.-Colonel.
David Stewart . . .	18 Apr. 1822	4 Dec. 1828	Exchanged to 65th Foot.
William Moore‡ . . .	20 Mar. 1823	31 Jan. 1828	Retired.
Eyre John Crabbe . .	31 Jan. 1828	6 Nov. 1841	Promoted Lieut.-Colonel.
John William Hutchinson	4 Dec. 1828	22 Oct. 1830	Died.
Donald John McQueen .	23 Oct. 1830	3 Oct. 1834	Retired.
Thomas Mannin . . .	3 Oct. 1834	12 Oct. 1839	Died at sea.
William White Crawley	13 Oct. 1839	1 May 1846	Promoted Lieut.-Colonel.
John Casamir Harold .	6 Nov. 1841	22 Oct. 1844	Exchanged to 11th Foot.
John Fordyce . . .	22 Oct. 1844	10 July 1846	Promoted Lieut.-Colonel.
Augustus Francis Ansell	1 May 1846	..	..
Hon. Thomas O'Grady .	10 July 1846	..	..

* Brevet Lieut.-Colonel. † Brevet Lieut.-Colonel, 30th June, 1813.
‡ Brevet Major, 21st June, 1813.

APPENDIX

TO THE

HISTORICAL RECORD

OF

THE SEVENTY-FOURTH REGIMENT,

(HIGHLANDERS.)

No. 1.

A monument was erected in the year 1795, in Poet's Corner, Westminster Abbey, to the memory of Major-General Sir ARCHIBALD CAMPBELL, who raised the SEVENTY-FOURTH HIGHLANDERS, which bears the following inscription :—

" Sacred to the memory of Major-General Sir Archibald Campbell, Knight of the Bath, Colonel of the SEVENTY-FOURTH Highland Regiment of Foot, Hereditary Usher of the White Rod in Scotland, late Governor of Jamaica, Governor of Fort St. George, and Commander-in-Chief of the Forces on the Coast of Coromandel, in the East Indies. He died equally regretted and admired for his eminent civil and military services to his country; possessed of distinguished endowments of mind, dignified manners, inflexible integrity, unfeigned benevolence, with every social and amiable virtue. He departed this life March 31st, 1791. Aged 61."

No. 2.

Lieut.-Colonel CAMPBELL, afterwards Lieut.-General Sir Alexander Campbell, Baronet, and K.C.B., entered the service as Ensign in the 1st battalion of Royals, in the year 1776, was promoted to a Lieutenancy in 1778, to a company in the 97th regiment by purchase in 1780, in the course of that year served on board a ninety-gun ship, belonging to the Channel

Fleet, under Admiral Darby, in command of three companies of his regiment. In 1781 the 97th was landed at Gibraltar, where he commanded the light company during the remainder of the siege.

At the peace of 1783 he was placed on half-pay. Being appointed as Captain to the SEVENTY-FOURTH on its formation in 1787, he raised nearly five hundred men for the regiment; he went to India in 1793, and in the following year was appointed Brigade-Major to the King's troops on the Coast of Coromandel, and subsequently in the same year, was selected by Lord Hobart, Governor of Madras, for the civil, judicial, and military charge of the settlement and fort of Pondicherry, recently conquered from the French, and was honoured with the expression of the entire approbation of Government for his services therein. He was promoted to a regimental Majority on the 1st of September, and to a Lieutenant-Colonelcy on the 4th of December, 1795. In the year 1797 he was appointed to command a flank corps of the force formed at Madras, to act against Manilla. The expedition, however, proceeded no further than Prince of Wales Island, whence it was recalled to Fort St. George.

In 1799, he commanded the SEVENTY-FOURTH in the army under General Harris, and received the thanks of the Commander-in-Chief for the gallant conduct of the corps at the battle of Mallavelly. At the siege and capture of Seringapatam, he was particularly distinguished by the strongest expressions of the Commander-in-Chief's approbation. He also served in the first campaign which immediately followed the conquest of Mysore against Dhoondia Waugh, under Sir Arthur Wellesley.

In 1800, he was appointed to the command of the fort of Bangalore, which he retained until he was removed to the command of Pondicherry. In 1801, he was selected to command the force destined to reduce the Danish settlement of Tranquebar. In 1802, he was appointed to command the northern division of the Madras army, with a force of five thousand men, occupying a line of sea-coast seven hundred miles in length, and received the uniform approbation of his superiors in the conduct of various detachments of this force, employed in action and difficult operations; and in most unhealthy districts.

At the commencement of the war with the Mahratta States in 1803, the Marquis Wellesley, Governor-General, selected him to command the force, upwards of five thousand men, for the subjugation of the Province of Cuttack, the arrangements for which enterprise were entirely completed by him, but severe illness, which endangered his life for several weeks afterwards, prevented him from leading the troops employed on this service, and he was obliged to return after the first day's march.

On the 25th of September this year, he obtained the rank of Colonel. In 1805, he was appointed to the command of Seringapatam, Mysore, and all of the late Tippoo Sultaun's dominions, on the departure of Sir Arthur Wellesley from India. In 1806, on the return home of the SEVENTY-FOURTH, he was retained in India by the Commander-in-Chief, and appointed to the command of Trichinopoly and the southern division of the army, where a strong force had just been assembled for field service, General Macdoual being appointed to the command of Mysore; at this time he had the good fortune, by the means he adopted, to seize about two hundred of the mutineers engaged in the massacre of the European troops at Vellore.

Colonel Campbell left India towards the end of 1807, and on his arrival in England in 1808, he was appointed a Brigadier-General, and placed on the staff of the army in Ireland. In January, 1809, he was appointed to the staff of the army in the Peninsula, was present at the crossing of the Douro, and in the pursuit of Marshal Soult. He commanded the division which formed the right wing of the British army at Talavera, where he was severely wounded through the thigh by a grapeshot. On this occasion, he received the marked approbation of the Commander-in-Chief, in orders, for his "courage and judgment," and was recommended by him for some substantial mark of His Majesty's favour; in consequence of which he was appointed Colonel of the York Light Infantry Volunteers. In January, 1810, being recovered from his wounds, he rejoined the army in Portugal, and was soon after appointed to command a division.

He was removed from the list of the SEVENTY-FOURTH by his promotion to the rank of Major-General on the 25th of July, 1810, up to which date he remained Lieut.-Colonel in the regiment, having served in it for twenty-two years, fifteen of them in the East Indies. On his leaving the regiment, he was the only individual who had belonged to it at its formation in 1787.

Major-General Campbell afterwards served in the Peninsula, in command of the sixth division, until severe illness compelled him to return to England in December, 1811 ; he was then employed as Commander of the Forces at the Mauritius, was promoted to Lieut.-General in the year 1814, and in the same year was created a Baronet, and received the Order of Knight Commander of the Bath, and was appointed Colonel of the 80th regiment in 1815.

Sir Alexander Campbell had three sons, and three nephews, officers in the SEVENTY-FOURTH ; of his sons, two (Lieutenants in the regiment,) were killed during the Mahratta campaign, one on detached service, and the other, Lieutenant John Morshead Campbell, at the battle of Assaye ; the third and only surviving son lived to be promoted to a Majority in the regiment in the year 1810, but died in November, 1813, of a wound received at the battle of the Pyrenees. Of his nephews, who were brothers of Lieutenant-General Sir Colin Campbell, K.C.B., (then Lieutenant in the 78th regiment,) Captain John Campbell and Lieutenant Alexander Campbell, were killed on detached service against the southern Polygars, in the beginning of 1801, at a siege where the storming party to which they belonged, being recalled from an impracticable breach, one of them having missed his brother, and being informed that he had fallen, returned to the breach and succeeded in bringing him off; but was also mortally wounded in doing so, and they both died in the same tent. The third and youngest of these brothers, Lieutenant Lorn Campbell, was killed at Assaye.

No. 3.

List of Officers of the Seventy-fourth Highlanders whose Deaths are recorded as having taken place during the service of the Regiment in the East Indies, between the Years 1790 *and* 1804.

RANK.	NAME	Date of Death.
Lieut.-Col.	Hamilton Maxwell	8 June 1794
,, ,,	Marlbro' Sterling.	4 December 1795
,, ,,	Alexander Ross	3 December 1796
Major	Francis Skelly	30 November 1793
Captain	Richard Eastland	12 October 1790
,,	James Clarke	19 August 1791
,,	John Campbell	31 October 1792
,,	John Campbell	16 July 1801
,,	James Campbell	2 May 1801
,,	Richard Neilson	19 September 1796
,,	Charles McKenzie	28 February 1800
,,	David Aytone	23 September 1803
,,	Andrew Dyce	23 September 1803
,,	Roderick McLeod	23 September 1803
,,	John Maxwell	23 September 1803
,,	Boswell Campbell	.. ..
Lieutenant	Dugald Lamont	8 November 1791
,,	John Forbes	12 November 1791
,,	John Gorrey	19 September 1791
,,	Peter Peaton	24 December 1790
,,	Alexander Stewart	29 May 1792
,,	James Campbell	6 December 1797
,,	John Wallace	29 November 1791
,,	Charles Campbell	24 October 1790
,,	John Campbell	28 June 1793
,,	John McGrigor	1 January 1796
,,	Stewart Douglas	7 May 1792
,,	Charles Abernethy	15 November 1795
,,	James Farquhar	4 May 1799
,,	Breon Fletcher	20 April 1803
,,	James Prendergast	4 May 1799
,,	George Campbell	10 August 1796
,,	John Campbell	23 September 1803
,,	Vesey Hill	4 May 1799
,,	John Morshead Campbell	23 September 1803
,,	Henry Shawe	4 May 1799
,,	Lewis Irvine	26 April 1799
,,	Dugald William Gilchrist	4 May 1801
,,	Alexander Campbell	1 April 1801
,,	James Grant	23 September 1803
,,	Patrick Shank	31 March 1801
,,	Thomas William Edwards	17 November 1799
,,	Robert Neilson	23 September 1803
,,	R. McMurdo	27 September 1803
,,	William Robertson	13 July 1801
,,	Lorn Campbell	23 September 1803
,,	Martin Morris	23 September 1803

No. 3—*continued.*

List of Officers of the Seventy-fourth Highlanders whose Deaths are recorded as having taken place in the East Indies, between the Years 1790 *and* 1804—continued.

RANK.	NAME.	Date of Death.
Ensign. .	John Gordon	31 March 1792
,,	James Leggett	19 January 1796
,,	W. M. Charleton.	.. ..
,,	Hugh Munro	6 November 1802
,,	Edward Bacon	17 October 1802
Volunteer .	—— Tew	23 September 1803
Ast. Surgeon	James Andrews	11 May 1804

No. 4.

State of the Seventy-fourth Highlanders on its embarkation for the Peninsula, 18th January, 1810.

DISTRIBUTION.	Colonel.	Lieut.-Colonel.	Majors.	Captains.	Lieutenants.	Ensigns.	Staff.	Serjeants.	Drummers.	Rank and File.	Women.	Children.
Embarked . . .	.	1	1	8	8	15	6	31	21	639	45	16
On Command . .	1	.	.	2	.	1	.	.	.	2	.	.
Recruiting . . .	.	.	.	.	4	1	.	8	.	27	.	.
Leave and Furlough	.	.	.	.	.	1	.	3	.	3	.	.
Sick, Absent . .	.	.	1	.	.	.	.	2	1	69	.	.
Absent without leave	.	.	.	.	.	.	.	.	.	7	.	.
Total Effectives.	1	1	2	10	12	18	6	44	22	747	.	.
Wanting to complete	.	.	.	.	.	2	.	.	.	53	.	.
Establishment . .	1	1	2	10	12	20	6	44	22	800	.	.

Rank and Names of the Officers who embarked for the Peninsula.

Lieut. Col. R. Le Poer Trench.
Major Manners.
Captain Langlands.
,, Mein.
,, Shawe.
,, Collins.
,, Moore.
,, Miller.
,, Thomson.
,, McNeill.
Lieutenant McQeeen.
,, Kennedy.
,, Cargill.
,, Maxwell.
,, Stuart.
,, Wingate.
,, Tew.
,, Crabbe.
Ensign Pattison.
,, Ewing.
Ensign Brown.
,, Grant.
,, Alves.
,, Collins.
,, King.
,, Graham.
,, Johnston.
,, Pye.
,, Nevin.
,, Heron.
,, Williams.
,, Ramadge.
,, Manning.
Surgeon Lindsay.
Assistant Surgeon Grant.
,, ,, Hamilton.
Pay-Master Hassard.
Adjutant Cresswell.
Quarter-Master Fraser

Officers Absent.

Colonel Sir Alexander Hope, Major-General (Deputy Quarter-Master General).
Lieut.-Colonel Alexander Campbell (Colonel, Brigadier-General).
Major Broughton, sick.
Captain Allen William Campbell, Assistant Adjutant-General, Portugal.
,, Hassard, sick.
Lieutenant Ansell, recruiting at Glasgow.
,, Robertson ,, Thurso.
,, Lyster ,, Lancaster.
,, Whitting ,, Athlone.
Ensign Douglass ,, Inverness.
,, Black, in charge of sick men at Cork.
,, Atkinson, newly appointed.

No. 5.

Establishment of the Seventy-fourth Highlanders, 25th October, 1810.
Eleven Companies.

1 Colonel.
1 Lieutenant-Colonel.
2 Majors.
11 Captains.
24 Lieutenants.
9 Ensigns.
1 Pay-Master.
1 Adjutant.
1 Quarter-Master.
1 Surgeon.
2 Assistant-Surgeons.
1 Serjeant-Major.
1 Quarter-Master-Serjeant.
1 Pay-Master-Serjeant.
1 Armourer-Serjeant.
58 Serjeants.
58 Corporals.
24 Drummers.
2 Fifers.
950 Privates.

1,150 Total of all ranks, officers and men

Establishment of the Seventy-fourth Highlanders, 25th June, 1811.
Eleven Companies.

1 Colonel.
1 Lieutenant-Colonel.
2 Majors.
11 Captains.
24 Lieutenants.
9 Ensigns.
1 Pay-Master.
1 Adjutant.
1 Quarter-Master.
1 Surgeon.
2 Assistant Surgeons.
73 Serjeants.
68 Corporals.
26 Drummers
1,140 Privates.

1,361 Total of all ranks, officers and men.

Establishment of the Seventy-Fourth Highlanders, 25th Feb., 1815.
Ten Companies.

1 Colonel.
1 Lieutenant-Colonel.
2 Majors.
10 Captains.
22 Lieutenants.
8 Ensigns.
1 Pay-Master.
1 Adjutant.
1 Quarter-Master.
1 Surgeon.
2 Assistant-Surgeons.
45 Serjeants.
40 Corporals.
22 Drummers.
760 Privates.

917 Total of all ranks, officers and men.

Establishment of the Seventy-fourth Highlanders, 1st January, 1818.
Eleven Companies.

1 Colonel.
1 Lieutenant-Colonel.
2 Majors.
11 Captains
14 Lieutenants.
8 Ensigns.
1 Pay-Master.
1 Adjutant.
1 Quarter-Master.
1 Surgeon.
2 Assistant Surgeons.
53 Serjeants.
48 Corporals.
22 Drummers.
760 Privates.

926 Total of all ranks, officers, and men.

No. 6.

Nominal Returns of Non-commissioned Officers and Men who are recorded as having been Killed or Wounded on the undermentioned occasions in the Peninsula and France.

At Busaco, 27th September, 1810.

Killed.

Private Richard Green.
,, John Dick.
,, Thomas Rowen.
,, John Lee.
,, Wm. McIntosh.
,, James Fitzpatrick.
,, Connor Minton.

Wounded.

Serjeant J. Abbott.
Private Francis Hand.
,, Alexander Hislop.
,, Andrew McNee.
,, William Campbell.
,, John Ross.
,, James Watson.
,, William Palmer.
,, David Dalgleish.
,, William Duncan.
,, Angus Campbell.
,, George Bogle.
,, Lawrence Byrne.
,, Patrick Carroll.
,, Richard Creighton.
,, James McCally.
,, John Mulholland.
,, William Hardy.
,, John McGiffort

At Redinha, 21st March. 1811.

Killed.

Private Andrew Egleton

Wounded.

Private Joseph Lesslie.
,, John Kelly.
,, John Middleton.
,, Robert McEwen.
,, Thomas Minnis.
,, Richard Nicholson.

At Fuentes d'Onor, 5th May, 1811.

Killed

Serjeant Ballingal.
Corporal Miller.
Private Alexander Williamson.
,, Patrick Woods.

Wounded.

Serjeant Hall.
Corporal Dallas.
,, McDonald.
,, Ross.
,, Gibb.
,, Campbell.
Private Robert Long.
,, Thomas Newton.
,, Arthur Graham.
,, Matthew Kidd.
,, William Charleton.
,, Angus Cameron.
,, Denis Galagher.
,, Alexander McClellan.
,, James Forester.
,, William Miller (2).
,, John Green.
,, Daniel Kelly.
,, James Carter.
,, James Clarke.
,, James Marquis.

Private Alexander Cannon.
,, George Gordon.
,, Patrick Bradley.
,, Robert Cunningham.
,, John McKenzie.
,, Ponts. Campbell.
,, Patrick Callaghan.
,, Derby Fechan.
,, David Weston.
,, Colin Matheson.
,, C. Kane.
,, William Clifton.
,, C. Brinen.
,, John Reilly.
,, Peter Murray.
,, Charles Caldoo.
,, Ralph Little.
,, Inps. Little.
,, Robert McFarlane.
,, Thomas Mooney.
,, John Smith.
,, Samuel McDonald.
,, John McLisky.
,, Henry O'Hara.
,, Thomas Crawley.
,, George Berry.
,, John McKenzie.
,, Andrew McKenzie.
,, John McDonald.
,, Lauty Collins.
,, William McCallum.

SIEGE OF CIUDAD RODRIGO,
4th to 19th January, 1812.

Killed.

Corporal McLanaghan.
Private George Hay.
,, Simon Fraser.
,, David Dalziel.
,, David McCann.
,, John Waterhouse.

Wounded.

Serjeant McLeod.
Corporal Connon.
,, McPherson.
,, Fitzsimons.
,, Henderson.
Private Donald Fraser.
Private Andrew McCulloch.
,, James Tanner.
,, Hugh Mulholland.
,, Felix Murphy.
,, Joseph Johnston.
,, Michael Callaghan.
,, John Parker.
,, John Ross.
,, Daniel Sleaven.
,, Robert McIntyre.
,, Robert McPherson.
,, John Taylor.
,, John Marmion.
,, John Donoghoe.
,, Donald McLeod.
,, John Sheridan.
,, George Brown.
,, Henry Ashburry.
,, John Graham.
,, Patrick Milligan.

SIEGE OF BADAJOZ,
16th March to 7th April, 1812.

Killed.

Serjeant Strachan.
Corporal John Curry.
,, D. McLeod.
Private Robert Buchanan.
,, Alex. Campbell (1st).
,, John McIntyre.
,, William Dunsmore.
,, William McDonnell.
,, James Gilmore.
,, James Todd.
,, George Robertson.
,, Munro McKay.
,, David McClure.
,, John Kirk.
,, Hugh Hughes.
,, John Carfull.
,, William Hadden.
,, Donald Grant.
,, James Sutherland.
,, Alexander Stewart.
,, John Fraser.
,, David Sinclair.
,, John McGill.
,, Francis Mohan.
,, Moore Halloran.

Wounded.

Serjeant George Robertson.
,, Jordan.
,, Mallard.
,, White.
,, Reagan.
Lance Serjeant J. Russell.
Corporal Aughterloine.
,, Cameron.
,, McKissock.
,, G. Forbes.
,, B. McGuire.
Private Thomas Pierce.
,, George Taylor.
,, James Wood.
,, James Shawe.
,, Joseph Green.
,, Andrew Clark.
,, Thomas Davidson.
,, John Fisken.
,, Alexander Hughes.
,, Laurence Hughes.
,, William Jamieson.
,, David Little.
,, George McCann.
,, John McGiffort.
,, James Reilley.
,, James Shanks.
,, James White.
,, Alexander Whitside.
,, Michael Butler.
,, John Davis.
,, Michael Kennedy.
,, Patrick Lee.
,, Bernard McLean.
,, William Murray.
,, George Gordon.
,, Jeremiah Murphy.
,, Robert Anderson.
,, Alexander Cameron.
,, Thomas Caulfield.
,, Evan Evans.
,, Thomas Johnston.
,, James Marshall.
,, George Robertson.
,, Henry Hart.
,, Robert Boyde.
,, William Thomas.
,, Joseph Tosh.
,, John Vasey.
Private William Gormley.
,, John Hair.
,, John Wilson.
,, John McEwan.
,, Daniel McGlone.
,, Thomas Finegan.
,, Joseph Lamoon.
,, James McEwen.
,, Timothy Flannery.
,, John Lynn.
,, James Gordon.
,, Michael Conway.
,, Bernard Monaghan.
,, David Falls.
,, Andrew Steadsman.
,, Luke Hill.
,, John McClernan.
,, Thomas Woodward.
,, William Weeks.
,, George Thomson.
,, William Downie.
,, George McPherson.
,, James Winter.
,, John Henderson.
,, Neil McFarlane.
,, James Wilson.
,, William Petrie.
,, Samuel Bridget.
,, James Dillon.
,, George Burns.
,, Samuel Taylor.
,, James McPherson.
,, Edward Powell.
,, Michael Lally.
,, Alexander Grant.
,, Robert Wright.
,, John Hyland.
,, Alexander Fife.
,, Alexander McLeod.
,, Edward Ryan.
,, Thomas Campbell.

At Salamanca,
22nd July, 1812.

Killed.

Lance Serjeant Dallas.
Private Patrick Coddy.
,, Val. Garland.

Wounded.

Serjeant Barr.
,, Sinclair.
Corporal Porter.
,, Miller.
,, Roy.
Private Alexander Jess.
,, Hugh Griffin.
,, Timothy Desmond.
,, Thomas Dunn.
,, Evan Morgan.
,, Henry McInally.
,, George McKenzie.
,, Daniel Tawney.
,, Thomas Kennedy.
,, Bernard Burke.
,, Robert Brown.
,, William Milligan.
,, William Adams.
,, Robert Patterson.
,, James Stewart.
,, Thomas Wilson.
,, Thomas Davidson.
,, James Dooland.
,, John Loughnan.
,, Thomas Keating.
,, Francis McCabe.
,, James O'Neill.
,, William Hodge.
,, William Gibb.
,, Patrick Bradley.
,, David Finniston.
,, Michael Naughton.
,, James Armstrong.
,, Philip Smith.
,, William Rodds.
,, John Rees.
,, William Chatburn.
,, Samuel Smith.
,, Quintin Logan.
,, Simon Barry.
,, George Beatley.
,, David Curry.
,, Thomas Ewart.
,, James Hunter.

At Vittoria,
21st June, 1813.

Killed.

Private James McCulloch.
,, John McLauchlan.
,, David Dalglish.
,, William Murray.
,, Thomas Carr.
,, George McKenzie.
,, John Irish.

Wounded.

Serjeant-Major McPherson.
Serjeant W. Ross.
,, Morrison.
,, Bassill.
Drummer James Kincaid.
Corporal J. Taylor.
,, D. McGurk.
Private John Brooker.
,, Owen McIntee.
,, Phenon McKinnon.
,, James O'Hara.
,, Philip Smith.
,, Michael Kirnan.
,, Owen Kennedy.
,, Peter Kane.
,, Thomas Power.
,, Darby Cooligha.
,, Peter Ballard.
,, John Cramp.
,, Patrick Hughes.
,, Thomas Cunningham.
,, Michael Errolls.
,, Patrick Muldoon.
,, Charles Mulholland.
,, James Gordon.
,, Patrick Houlighan.
,, Matthew Briggs.
,, George Beecroft.
,, William Houston.
,, Thomas Crawley.
,, Walter O'Neill.
,, Patrick Heavey.
,, John Dunn.
,, George Nave.
,, Thomas Banco.
,, Samuel Parkinson.

BEFORE PAMPELUNA.

15th July, 1813.

Killed.

William Smith.
William Harwood.
Philip Pratt.

Wounded.

Serjeant Reid.
Corporal Sharky.
Private John McEwen.
,, Robert McFarlane.
,, Thomas Brown.
,, Richard Bishop.
,, Thomas Forrest.

ACTION NEAR PAMPELUNA.

30th July, 1813.

Killed.

Serjeant Holler.
Private Alexander Campbell.
,, Charles Jelly.
,, George Stewart.
,, Robert Wallace.

Wounded.

Serjeant J. Jervis.
,, Biggar.
,, Duncan.
,, Sinclair.
Corporal P. Wilson.
,, W. Nichol.
,, D. Fleming.
Private Alexander Buchanan.
,, William Devlin.
,, Duncan Dunbar.
,, John Falloon.
,, James Gibson.
,, David Henry.
,, John McGregor.
,, James Grear.
,, Henry Pye.
,, Joseph McCreary.
,, John McBride.
,, Cornelius Caulfield.
,, Alexander McKnight.
,, John Kelly.
,, John McPherson.
,, Roderick McDonald.
,, John Barry (1st).
Private Thomas Banco.
,, David Cargill.
,, John Kearney.
,, Donald Johnston.
,, Henry Graham.
,, James Blackrae.
,, George McPherson.
,, Hector McRae.
,, Robert Cunningham.
,, John Graham.
,, Patrick Lee.
,, James Martin.
,, Michael Mossey.
,, Jeremiah Murphy.
,, Lawrence O'Brien.
,, Patrick Reagan.

AT ORTHES.

27th February, 1814.

Killed.

Serjeant Mallard.
Corporal Montgomery.
Private Patrick McGill.
,, Hugh McLoughlin.
,, Michael Mossey.
,, John Stewart.
,, Peter Stewart.
,, George Williams.

Wounded.

Serjeant Quince.
Drummer Donald McKenzie.
Corporal Campbell.
,, Raymond.
,, McDonald.
,, Ross.
Private Michael Fallon.
,, Alexander Lamb.
,, Peter Lee.
,, John Mulholland.
,, William Longmore.
,, Joseph Leaver.
,, William Wassal.
,, Daniel McKenzie.
,, Angus McLean.
,, Patrick Muldoon.
,, John Burke.
,, Thomas Forest.
,, Hugh Gordon.
,, Charles Peet.

AT TOULOUSE,
10th April, 1814.

Killed.

Serjeant Fleming.
Corporal Angus.
,, W. Jordan.
,, D. Merson.
,, John Spratt.
,, Dugald McQueen.
,, John Syms.
Private William Charnock.
,, James Walker.
,, John Gribble.
,, John Sheridan.
,, Michael Butler.
,, Duncan Chisholm.
,, James Nelson.
,, Thomas Forrest.
,, Henry Martin.
,, Samuel Anderson.
,, William McKay.
,, Roderick Young.
,, John Calcrith.
,, David Clifton.
,, Henry Holden.
,, Michael Conway.
,, David Falls.
,, William Ford.
,, Charles Lees.
,, James Morrison.
,, George Thomson.
,, William Cliff.
,, James McEwen.
,, Angus Kelly.
,, James Fox
,, John Smith.

Wounded.

Serjeant-Major McPherson.
Serjeant William Miller.
,, James McLean.
,, William Graham.
Corporal Nimmo Roy.
,, James McKeever.
,, James Adge.
Private David Arthur.
,, Burke Barnot.
,, Archibald McGill.
,, Peter Turnbull.
,, Thomas Nelson.
,, Daniel Towney.
,, John McBride.
,, Richard Brown.
,, Alexander Hardie.
,, Laurence Kane.
,, William Olliver.
,, John Verinda.
,, John Millikin.
,, Bernard McKnight.
,, Hugh Mitchell.
,, Thomas Naughton.
,, John Bone.
,, George Stewart.
,, Patrick Buchanan.
,, Robert Dickson.
,, John Dornon.
,, George Gyte.
, Evan Lloyd.
,, Owen McGleevie.
,, Angus McLean.

NOTE.—These nominal returns are defective, the names of many men killed and wounded in the different actions, particularly at Toulouse, have not been inserted; and of the casualties in several of the minor affairs, there is no record now with the regiment.

No. 7.

Statement by Town Major White, dated "Portsmouth, 6th July, 1848," of the occurrences observed by him, as Lieutenant and Adjutant of the Seventy-fourth, at the Battle of Busaco.

At the battle of Busaco the SEVENTY-FOURTH were stationed, together with two field-pieces, under Major Arentschildt, of the Portuguese service, across a road leading over the mountain; the guns did much destruction to the enemy, and the fire which they drew in return did much execution in the ranks of the SEVENTY-FOURTH regiment without its fire being able to reach the enemy in retaliation. Various desperate attacks were made by them (the enemy) to carry the hill in several places, but failed, as we witnessed, with much anxiety, until the afternoon, when they advanced more determinedly, and with greater numbers, to force the road which the SEVENTY-FOURTH protected, and it appeared we were by no means in numbers to resist them; a space being vacated on our left by a Portuguese regiment made our situation very desperate, which it appears was observed by the Fifth Division from a distant height, and General Leith sent two regiments with yellow facings (I think the ninth and thirty-eighth) to meet the enemy in this gap; they came at double-quick time along our rear from the right, and wheeled round in close column on our left, meeting the head of a mass of the French in close contact, who were advancing up the hill and likely to turn our left. This contact was so immediate, and the hill so steep, that the brigade of the Fifth Division had not time to deploy, but literally ran down upon the enemy in close column, or nearly so; the SEVENTY-FOURTH moving forward with them part of the way; this decided the fate of the day, for the enemy never advanced afterwards. I mention this, because I have somewhere read that the Third Division was giving way when the Fifth Division came down; this was not the case, the SEVENTY-FOURTH never retreated a step the whole day, but advanced at last as above stated. I was near the left of the regiment at the moment the brigade of the Fifth Division arrived, and from the smoke and confusion I think the movement has not been clearly noticed by many besides myself, as I have frequently spoken to officers about it, who I found had not observed it. The brigade of the Fifth Division came so hurriedly into action that they did not observe our position, and we, with an enemy forcing our front, did not observe them.

No. 8.

Extract from Major Alves's Journal regarding the attack upon the tête-de-pont by the Seventy fourth Regiment, and Major-General Sir Thomas Brisbane's Brigade of the Third Division, at Toulouse on the 10th of April, 1814.

"Shortly after daylight the division was put in motion, with orders to drive all the enemy's out-posts before us, and although acting as Adjutant, I was permitted by Colonel Trench to accompany the skirmishers; with but feeble opposition we drove them before us, until they reached the *tête-de-pont* on the canal leading into Toulouse, on the right bank of the Garonne; on arriving there I mentioned to Captain Andrews of the SEVENTY-FOURTH, that I thought we had gone far enough, and reconnoitred very attentively the manner in which it was defended by strong palisades, &c.; I then returned to where the regiment was halted, and mentioned my observations to Colonel Trench, and that nothing further could possibly be done without artillery to break down the palisades. He immediately brought me to General Brisbane, to whom I also related my observations as above, who directed me to ride to the left and find out Sir Thomas Picton, who was with the other brigade, and to tell him my observations. After riding about two miles to the left I found Sir Thomas, and told him as above stated, who immediately said, in presence of all his staff, 'Go back, Sir, and tell them to move on.' This I did with a very heavy heart, as I dreaded what the result must be, but I had no alternative. About a quarter of an hour afterwards the regiment moved from where it was halted. We experienced a loss of thirty killed and one hundred wounded, out of three hundred and fifty, in the attempt to get possession of the *tête-de-*

pont; and were obliged to retire without gaining any advantage. The attack was the more to be regretted, as Lord Wellington's orders were that it was only to be a diversion and not a real attack."

No. 9.

General Order by Field-Marshal the Duke of Wellington, referred to at page 102 *of the Regimental Records.*

Bordeaux, 14*th June,* 1814.

General Order.

1. The Commander of the Forces being upon the point of returning to England, again takes this opportunity of congratulating the Army upon the recent events which have restored peace to their country and to the world.

2. The share which the British army have had in producing those events, and the high character with which the army will quit this country, must be equally satisfactory to every individual belonging to it, as they are to the Commander of the Forces, and he trusts that the troops will continue the same good conduct to the last.

3. The Commander of the Forces once more requests the Army to accept his thanks.

4. Although circumstances may alter the relations in which he has stood towards them for some years so much to his satisfaction, he assures them he will never cease to feel the warmest interest in their welfare and honor, and that he will be at all times happy to be of any service to those to whose conduct, discipline, and gallantry their country is so much indebted.

No. 10.

Officers of the Seventy-fourth Highlanders upon whom rewards of Brevet rank, Gold Medals, or Decorations, were conferred for special services during the Peninsular War.

Regimental Rank and Name.	*Distinctions conferred.*
Lieut.-Colonel Hon. Robert Le Poer Trench	Gold cross and clasp, K.C.B.
Major Russell Manners. . . .	Brevet of Lieut.-Colonel, gold cross and C.B.
,, Allen William Campbell .	Brevet of Lieut.-Colonel, gold medal.
Captain George Langlands . .	Brevet of Major, gold medal and clasp.
,, Matthew Shawe . . .	Brevets of Major and Lieut.-Colonel, gold medal and C B.
,, William Moore . . .	Brevet of major.
,, James Miller	Brevet of major, gold cross.
,, Alexander Thomson . .	Brevets of major and Lieut.-Colonel, gold medal and C.B.

No. 11.

Copy of a Letter from the Adjutant-General of the Forces to Lieut.-General Sir Phineas Riall, K.C.B., Colonel of the Seventy-fourth regiment, referred to at page 110.

"*Horse Guards,*
"Sir, 13*th August*, 1845.

"Having had the honor to submit to the Commander-in-Chief your letter of the 21st of June last, with its enclosures, I have it in command to acquaint you, that under the circumstances represented in these documents, his Grace will recommend to Her Majesty, that the Seventy-fourth regiment may be permitted to resume the appellation of "Highland Regiment," and to be clothed accordingly; that is, to wear the tartan trews instead of the Oxford mixture, plaid cap instead of the black chaco, and the plaid scarf as worn by the seventy-first regiment.

"Although the Commander-in-Chief has thus consented to support the application of the officer commanding the Seventy-fourth, in compliment to the services of that regiment, (so well known to his Grace in India and in Europe) his Grace cannot keep out of view the fact, that it is found very difficult to complete the Highland regiments already on the establishment of the army with Highland, or even Scotch recruits; and that this state of things has rendered it occasionally necessary to extend their recruiting to other parts of the United Kingdom.

"As, however, Lieutenant-Colonel Crabbe holds out sanguine expectations of being able to keep up the establishment of the Seventy-fourth regiment by means of its local influences in Scotland, the Commander-in-Chief yields to the Lieutenant-Colonel's assurances under that head; but this with the distinct understanding, that should these expectations be disappointed, the expedients resorted to in the cases of other Highland regiments, similarly circumstanced, will be resorted to in the case of the Seventy-fourth regiment; that is, its efficiency as to numbers must be maintained from time to time by the other means alluded to, if that indispensable object cannot be attained by the exertions of its own recruiting parties in Scotland.

"I have the honor to be, Sir,
"Your most obedient humble Servant,
(Signed) "John Macdonald,
"*Adjutant-General.*"

No. 12.

List and Dates of the principal Battles, Sieges, and Affairs with the Enemy in which the Seventy-fourth Highlanders were engaged during the Peninsular War from 1810 *to* 1814.

[*Honorary distinctions have been granted for the services which have numbers prefixed.*]

1810.

No.	Event	Date
1	Battle of Busaco	27th September.

1811.

No.	Event	Date
	Affairs of Pombal	11th March.
	——— Redinha. . . .	12th ditto.
	——— Casal Novo. . .	14th ditto.
	——— Foz d'Aronce . .	15th ditto.
	——— Sabugal. . . .	3rd April.
2	Battle of Fuentes d'Onor . .	3rd and 5th May.
	Siege (second) of Badajoz. .	30th May to 13th June.
	Affairs of El Bodon . . .	25th September.
	——— Aldea de Ponte. .	27th ditto.

1812.

No.	Event	Date
3	Siege and Storm of Ciudad Rodrigo	(Captured 19th January,) 8th to 19th January.
4	Siege and Storm of Badajoz (third)	Escalade of Fort Picurina 25th March; escalade and capture of Badajoz 6th April . . . } 17th March to 6th April.
5	Battle of Salamanca . . .	22nd July.
	Occupation of Madrid . . .	12th August (Fort Retiro, Madrid, capitulated 14th August.)
	Affairs on the retreat from Madrid	3rd October to 19th November.

1813.

No.	Event	Date
6	Battle of Vittoria	21st June.
7	Battles of the Pyrenees . .	27th, 28th, and 30th July.
8	Battle of Nivelle	10th November.
9	——— the Nive	9th to 13th December.

1814.

No.	Event	Date
10	Battle of Orthes	27th February.
	Affair of Vic Bigorre . . .	19th March.
	——— Tarbes	20th ditto.
11	Battle of Toulouse	10th April.

No. 13.

List of Officers who have received Silver War Medals under the General Order of the 1st June, 1847, for their services in the Seventy-fourth Highlanders.

RANK and NAMES.	Rank in the Seventy-fourth during the War.	Reference to Services with the Seventy-fourth Regiment.	Remarks.
Major-General Alexander Thomson, C.B.	Captain	1, 2, 3, 4, 5, 6, 8, 9, 10*	
Lieut.-Colonel Russell Manners, C.B.	Major	1, 2, 3, 4, 5, 10, 11	
,, Eyre J. Crabbe, K.H.	Lieutenant	1, 3, 4, 5, 8, 9, 10, 11	Retired on full pay from command of the regiment, 1st May, 1846.
Major William Moore	Captain	1, 2, 4, 5, 6, 7	Retired.
,, Donald John McQueen, K.H.	,,	1, 2, 5, 6, 7, 8, 9, 10, 11	Retired, 1834. Barrack-master, Drogheda.
,, St. George Lyster	,,	2, 3, 4, 10	Retired.
,, †John Alves	Lieutenant	1, 2, 3, 4, 5, 6, 7, 8, 9, 10, 11	Depôt battalion.
Captain William Cargill	Captain	1, 6, 7, 8, 9, 10, 11.	Retired.
,, Lachlan McPherson	Serjeant-Major.	1, 2, 3, 4, 6, 7, 8, 10, 11	Captain unattached; Staff Officer of Pensioners.
Lieutenant John Black	Lieutenant.	6, 7, 8, 9, 10, 11	Fort Major, Kinsale.
,, James Fleetwood	,,	3, 4, 5, 8, 10, 11	Half pay, 25th Dragoons.
,, Richard Davies	,,	4, 5, 6, 7, 8, 10, 11	Paymaster; half pay, 74th Reg.
,, John Ormsby Lloyd	Ensign.	8, 9, 10, 11	Half pay, staff officer of pensioners.
Town Major Henry White	Adjutant	1, 2, 3, 5, 6	Died October, 1848.
Deputy Inspector Owen Lindsay, M.D.	Surgeon	1, 2, 5, 6, 7, 8, 9, 10, 11	
Quarter-Master Donald Fraser	Quarter-Master	1, 3, 6, 7	Retired full pay.

* The numbers placed opposite to the names refer to the preceding List, No. 12, of Battles and Sieges at which the 74th regiment was engaged.

† Major Alves acted as Adjutant of the regiment at the siege of Badajoz and during the greater part of the year 1812; and from the battle of Vittoria, in June, 1813, until the end of the war.

www.ingramcontent.com/pod-product-compliance
Lightning Source LLC
LaVergne TN
LVHW052353100826
845147LV00013B/828

9781783317578